Also by Julian Richer

The Richer Way
The Ethical Capitalist

Our Housing Disaster

– and what we can do about it

BY JULIAN RICHER

WITH KATE MILLER

Published by Richer Publishing and Media
Richer House, Hankey Place, London SE1 4BB

ISBN 978-1-7385594-0-4
Printed and bound by Elle Media Group, Basildon, Essex.

Julian Richer is an English retail entrepreneur, philanthropist and author, best known as the founder and managing director of Richer Sounds, the UK's largest hi-fi retailer. He transferred control of his firm to its employees in 2019 and 15% of the profits from Richer Sounds are donated to charities.

From founding ACTS435 in 2009, an organisation helping people in need, he has gone on to set up ASB Help in 2013, a charity that supports victims of anti-social behaviour. In 2015 he founded Parallel Histories with Michael Davies, a history schoolteacher in Lancaster, who came up with the idea of teaching contentious subjects in 'parallel'. He also started TaxWatch in 2018, dedicated to the research and exposure of aggressive tax avoidance. In 2020, Julian launched Zero Hours Justice to support workers who have zero-hours contracts imposed on them against their will and the Good Business Charter, an accreditation scheme to encourage responsible business. In 2021, he launched The Fairness Foundation to attempt to address the core issues involved to make society fairer. In November 2023 he launched the Campaign for Social Justice with renowned lawyer and media personality, Peter Stefanovic.

Julian has been a columnist for *The Sunday Times* and has written several books, including *The Richer Way* and *The Ethical Capitalist.*

Kate Miller is a journalist and editor who has worked with Julian on a number of his books. She has reported on housing issues for *The Guardian, The Times, Inside Housing* and for Shelter's publications.

Acknowledgements

Top of the list is my wife Rosie, who has supported me through thick and thin. With infinite care for me, her support, patience and loyalty have been above and beyond… I am very blessed.

Kate Miller, my writing partner going back to *The Richer Way* days in the early nineties, must take a big chunk of credit too. She's taken my initial miscellaneous ideas and notes, knocked them into shape and backed them up by digging into the research. They should now make much more sense for the general public, so huge thanks to her.

I would also like to thank some of the marketing team at Richer Sounds who have put this together, from the cover design, layout and proofreading to getting it printed: Claudia Vernon, Lol Lecanu and Rosie Wills.

Two people close to me kindly sanity-checked the proofs to hopefully prevent me making a fool of myself: David Robinson, my very wise, lifetime colleague, who is both chair of Richer Sounds and managing director of my property company, and Niki Adams, one of the many inspiring women at the Crossroads Women's Centre, so big thanks to them too.

Contents

Introduction

Far too many people in this country cannot afford a decent roof over their heads – a growing scandal that is having huge social consequences.

As a businessman who has had an active involvement with social housing and as a landlord myself, I've seen this problem grow, read numerous reports exposing the shocking facts and seen housing ministers come and go (15 since 2010!) – while little gets done.

This book has been a long time in the making. It was born in 2017 when I wrote a paper on social housing for the then shadow chancellor, John McDonnell. It started as a hotchpotch of observations and suggestions based on my 40 years of experience as a property owner, now with a sizeable property portfolio, but my frustration with the status quo pushed me to keep my thoughts alive and develop them further. Meanwhile, I could see the housing crisis getting worse, until it is now nothing less than a disaster.

Housing is a fundamental necessity for all of us, but it is a huge subject. Here in this book, I don't intend to cover all aspects of housing in the UK but want to focus on the most challenging and least glamorous sector, which is social housing. This is where I see the biggest problem for society, in that it's the most neglected sector, where there has been the least progress, causing the most suffering and affecting so many people in need of a decent and genuinely affordable place to live. It is also the sector where, I believe, the best solutions to our housing disaster lie.

Every year, as the gap between stagnant wages and rising house prices grows, fewer and fewer people can buy their own home. Consequently, millions are in private rented housing, paying high prices for insecure tenancies and often unsuitable and poor-quality accommodation. A million more are on waiting lists for the dwindling number of council or housing association homes, and many more would like to join those lists if they could be deemed eligible.

Having a secure, affordable home is a vital anchor in people's lives – I might even argue it is a fundamental human right. It is surely something we expect in a modern democracy. By 'affordable' I mean genuinely affordable – where people can cover their housing costs through their earnings or through housing benefit, without getting into financial difficulties. I emphasise this because, as I'll come back to in this book, the word 'affordable' is frequently used in the housing sector in a very misleading way, referring to homes that are not at all within the reach of people on low, or even average, incomes.

Politicians' responses to the growing housing disaster have been feeble. They are fixated on home ownership and, currently, Labour's main policy on housing is a claim that it will get the home ownership rate back up to 70%.[1]

But let's drop this fantasy and face reality. For there to be a surge in homebuying, young people's wages would have to shoot up, or house prices would have to plummet, or the taxpayer would have to finance huge state 'help to buy' subsidies. None of these seem likely. The only other way would be for families to cripple themselves financially, taking on a massive burden of debt if they were allowed to borrow more than five times their earnings, or locked into immensely long mortgages. Would that be good for them?

As I'll set out in this book, there are 8m people in this country in housing need, plus millions more who have a roof over their head in the private rented sector but live with the fear of arbitrary eviction or rents rising beyond their reach. Vote-catching promises about increasing home ownership are not going to bring these people any closer to a secure home, in good condition, that they can afford.

I want a better deal for them.

We have a housing disaster on our hands. This book argues that the only way to tackle it is with a new mindset, decisive action, and cash. There is no escaping that the government will have to invest money, but in the long term there will also be huge savings, plus a gain in state assets. We need to recognise that providing good-quality, rented housing, let on secure tenancies, at rents people can afford, is the only way to address society's immediate, urgent needs. We must acknowledge that this calls for state intervention – that the housing this country needs as a priority is what we'd broadly call 'social housing': homes to rent that have not been developed for profit. We need to admit that dismantling the supply of council housing, through a combination of underinvestment and the Right to Buy, has created a real social crisis.

Policymakers have already recognised that the UK has an undersupply of housing and that many more homes need to be built over the next decade. My argument is that boosting the supply cannot be simply left to the market. All that will happen is a repeat of what has taken place over the past 20 years, with house prices moving further and further out of reach for ordinary working people and nothing done for those who will never be able to buy.

In this book I look at how bad things are, how

Britain got into this mess and what we can do to find practical ways forward. There is much that can be done if there is the will and if we can get rid of the legal and financial restrictions preventing the supply of genuinely affordable homes.

I'm calling on politicians, local authorities, and private landlords to have the courage to act, and to get this country out of the mire of bad housing that is causing misery for millions.

CHAPTER 1

Disaster? What housing disaster?

Look at the TV schedule on any day and you can see how much an English person's home is their castle.

Escape to the Country, DIY SOS, Grand Designs, Love Your Garden, The Restoration Man, Location Location Location, Homes under the Hammer, Your Home Made Perfect, Love It or List It, Flipping Fast…

All these programmes – and countless column inches of newspaper and magazine articles – create the illusion that we are a nation of eager entrepreneurial homeowners, improving our homes and gardens, buying and selling, moving up the property ladder, 'flipping' properties by buying cheap, doing them up and selling at a profit. Property is a route to making money or 'escaping' to the lovely British countryside or the even lovelier (and warmer) Spanish, Greek or French countryside.

The word 'renting' is barely mentioned. There's no acknowledgement of the fact that thousands of people live in the kind of private rented accommodation where they are not even allowed to hang a picture on the wall.

Property programmes have always been about fantasy, but the fantasy is getting further and further away from reality. Large – and growing – sections of the population, particularly people on low incomes and younger generations, are not on any kind of property ladder. In fact, they have almost no prospect of getting on the bottom rung, which moves further out of their reach every year.

Yet there has been a national silence about the needs of people who are not homeowners.

Ever since the early 1980s when Margaret Thatcher's government introduced the Right to Buy for council tenants, the focus has been on home ownership as the only worthwhile goal. Creating a 'property-owning democracy' became something of a moral crusade, with an implicit suggestion that those who owned their own homes were 'better' people than those who did not. It's true that the ability to own one's home did open up genuine opportunities for millions, and gave them hope for the future, as they assumed future generations would continue to benefit. The politicians of the time hoped that owning their own homes would turn people into Conservative voters, which may or may not have been the case, but the effect was certainly to shift the balance on to owner-occupation as the sole measure of achievement – both for the individual and the nation.

The 1980s and 90s saw society become increasingly obsessed with property. Media headlines rejoiced every time property prices went up. There were hitches – many people found themselves in negative equity for a period in the early 90s – but this did not dent the underlying belief that people's homes should increase in value and that this was somehow making the nation wealthier.

Faith in the beneficial effects of house price inflation persists, despite the fact that people are well aware that rising house prices, combined now with much higher mortgage interest rates, are putting home ownership further and further out of reach for millions. Even *The Guardian*, which often questions conventional economic wisdom, couldn't resist the headline on 2 May 2023: 'UK house prices rise for first time in eight months, Nationwide expert hails "tentative signs of a recovery" as buyers' confidence improves'.

Falling or stagnant house prices are seen as a national 'ill' that we must recover from but, in fact, fast-rising house prices and interest rates have proved to be the real ill, destroying the dream of a property-owning democracy that was supposed to benefit all.

Britain's housing policy, such as it is, has failed on its own terms. To my eyes, for decades there hasn't been much of a policy beyond 'home ownership is best'. Of course, most people want to own their home, for very good reasons. For the moment, it is still the majority tenure and owning one's home should be a perfectly reasonable and legitimate aspiration. It is not for one generation (the comfortable homeowners) to tell younger generations that their wish to buy a home is foolish.

Yet the reality is that home ownership has fallen and is likely to fall further. For many people, a rise in house prices does not fill them with joy but makes their hearts sink as they see the possibility of getting a mortgage moving further out of reach. Meanwhile, many of those who have achieved home ownership by stretching themselves financially are finding their household budget crippled by higher interest rates and that their ability to pay the mortgage balances on a knife edge.

A brief look at the most basic outline figures shows why. The Nationwide survey referred to in the *Guardian* article found that the average price of a home rose to £260,441 in April 2023, from £257,122 in March.[1]

The Office for National Statistics (ONS) figures for average household incomes in the UK show that median household disposable income was £32,300 in the financial year ending 2022, a decrease of 0.6% from the previous financial year 2021.[2] The ONS measures income after tax, so that puts median gross household income at around £40,000. If, as a rough rule of thumb, a couple can borrow four times their combined salaries, that gets them a mortgage of £160,000.

These are broad-brush figures, but the basic problem is obvious: the gap between the price of a home and what a household could borrow to buy one is huge. It is unlikely to be bridged by the sort of savings a typical working family could accumulate.

Before the pandemic, about 40% of young working adults had no hope of buying one of the cheapest homes in their area, even with a 10% deposit, according to a study by the Institute for Fiscal Studies (IFS).[3] The IFS found house prices in England rose by 173% between 1996 and 2016, while average pay for 25-34-year-olds grew by 19% over the same period. The figure is likely to be higher than 40% now, with house prices having risen steeply since 2016. On average, a first-time buyer needs to put down a deposit of more than £60,000.[4]

This is a very different situation from that in which people found themselves up until the early 2000s, when having a regular salary allowed most people, and certainly most couples, to plan for buying their own home.

The government's figures, from its English Housing Survey 2021-22, show that owner-occupation, the largest housing tenure in England, has fallen from its peak of 71% in 2003 to 64% of all English households in 2021-22.[5] That adds up to 15.6m owner-occupier households.

Interestingly, the majority of owner-occupiers now own their homes outright: 35% of households compared to the 30% who are mortgagors. This very likely shows the generational gap that is opening up. People who bought in the 1980s and 90s have paid off their mortgages, while younger generations are finding it hard to enter the market.

It is obvious that things have changed since 2003, the peak of home ownership. We are in a new reality now and one that is not going to change in the short term. Incomes are not likely to shoot up and house prices to fall so that they meet in an ideal position of affordability.

Yet politicians are not responding to this new reality.

In recent years, the only thing resembling a policy has been a target for 300,000 new homes a year to be built (or converted from existing properties) in England, with repeatedly no mention of what sort of homes these would be – would they be privately owned, 'affordable' in some way or in the social rented sector?

The 300,000 new homes figure was set out in the Conservatives' 2019 manifesto, with the target to be reached 'in the mid 2020s'. The pandemic gave this aim a severe knock and things have not picked up since. The BBC's *Verify* report in November 2023[6] noted that in 2019-20 there were 248,591 net additional dwellings, which fell to 217,754 in 2020-21, partly due to the pandemic. It also noted that since the 1970s, on average 250,000 homes a year have been built; in some years this only added around a net 200,000 to the housing stock as others were demolished.

This is such a long-term trend that I would say it looks as if 250,000 homes a year is the figure the development and building industry is capable of – or perhaps comfortable with.

By December 2022, in the Levelling-Up and Regeneration Bill, the target had become a lot more vague. 'Housing targets remain, but they are a starting point with new flexibilities to reflect local circumstances,' said the press release from Michael Gove, Secretary of State for Housing and Communities.

According to the press release, the Bill put forward: 'new measures to strengthen commitment to building enough of the right homes in the right places with the right infrastructure'. This sounds reasonable, but is it anything more than a slogan?

The Labour Party is now also talking about its plans to get built '1.5m homes over the next Parliament' if it comes to power. As it happens, that equates to 300,000 homes a year, but there is no mention of whether these homes are social housing for rent, or just more properties for sale.

Not only do figures like the 300,000 target merely scratch the surface of the UK's housing problems, as I'll show, but the debate keeps coming back to the idea that buying and selling property solves everything.

Headline targets like '300,000 new homes' tend

to provoke reactions that create further obstacles to tackling the country's housing problems. There is frequently an immediate fear from communities that the new developments will be built on beloved green fields and that an influx of new residents will put further strain on already-stretched local services. Any mention of social housing being included in estates sparks rumours that this will bring down property prices. Rational discussion about housing needs gets lost in a bad-tempered welter of planning disputes, accusations of nimbyism, snobbery, and so on.

Interestingly, the 300,000 a year figure is not so much linked to analysis of housing need but was initially raised in the context of affordability.

Back in 2003, economist Kate Barker was commissioned by Labour's Chancellor Gordon Brown to investigate the reason for excessive house price inflation in the UK. She reported that housebuilding had fallen to its lowest point since the Second World War, and that the limited supply was pushing up prices. The number of new households that could afford to buy a home was dropping, while the number of homeless households in temporary accommodation was rising. She saw a direct link between supply and affordability: more homes needed to be built in order to stop house prices rising so fast.[7]

In subsequent years, as house price inflation rose ever higher, the figure for how many extra homes were needed in order to get back to some kind of affordability also rose. In 2017, when he was chancellor of the Exchequer, Philip Hammond said: 'Experts generally agree that to start to make inroads on the affordability programme, we've got to be sustainably delivering around 300,000 homes a year.'[8]

The figure was recommended by a House of Lords economic affairs committee report in 2016, which described it as the minimum annual amount needed to meet demand in England and 'have a moderating effect on house prices'.[9]

So the view has been that the affordability problem is a market problem: supply and demand are out of kilter. If only supply could be increased, house price increases would slow and become within reach for more people.

As we all know, since 2016 house prices have risen hugely while wages have continued to stagnate. The affordability problem is even more acute and increasing the supply of homes for sale is not going to make much of a dent in it, for many reasons. The 300,000 figure has become a meaningless mantra.

So far, leaving things to the market has provided no solutions.

The wider crisis

In a country obsessed with home ownership and house prices, genuine affordability is at the root of many people's housing woes, but it is only one aspect of a housing disaster that is harming the nation as a whole.

Poor-quality, overpriced housing is costing the taxpayer huge sums. For a start, let's note that the state pays out billions of pounds a year in housing benefit – £16.1bn in 2022-23 according to the National Audit Office[10] – because people, even if they are in work, cannot afford to pay the rents they are charged. That, in itself, says a lot about our housing crisis.

Poor housing is harming the nation's health. The housing ombudsman, Richard Blakeway, whose office deals with complaints from social housing tenants about disrepair and mould and damp in their homes, problems recognised now to be a threat to health, has found the situation to be so bad that he has called for a Royal Commission to look at the links between housing, health, and welfare.[11] Too often, the various agencies in housing, health and social care tend not to link up, or even know what the others are doing, which can end up making people's housing situation worse. Someone who has been homeless or who has mental health needs, for example, can require a lot of support once they are housed so that they can pay the rent and maintain the tenancy. If they just get housed and then left to cope on their own, they can struggle, lose the tenancy, become homeless and the whole cycle starts again, with all that waste of money and damage to lives.

Crises are coming to the boil now in every area of housing: in private renting and in the public sector, with local authorities unable to house homeless families, let alone anyone on their waiting list. Some councils have even officially declared a housing crisis, like Leicester City Council. It has 6,000 people on its waiting list and is seeing 5,000 people become homeless each year, but only about 900 of its homes become available to let annually, with about 350 properties a year being lost through Right to Buy. Elly Cutkelvin, Leicester's assistant mayor for housing, said, 'We have seen a tsunami of families presenting as homeless through section 21 eviction notices. It's wave after wave and there just aren't enough houses to go around. So we declared a crisis.'[12]

For people who have lost their homes, the crisis has turned into a nightmare, even if they are relatively lucky to have been given temporary accommodation. But many others are struggling with different kinds of housing stress.

Well-researched reports by numerous bodies come out every year, each drawing attention to another element in the housing crisis. In 2020, the National Housing Federation (NHF) – the trade body for housing associations (that is, social landlords) – pulled a lot of the issues together in its report *People in housing need: a comprehensive analysis of the scale and shape of housing need in England today.*[13]

The report concluded that nearly 8m people in England have some form of housing need. That finding was based on 2017-18 figures and can only have risen since, given the effects of the pandemic and the impact of interest rate rises, which have increased both mortgage repayments and, as a knock-on effect, rents in the private sector. The huge rise in energy prices in 2022 also created a crisis, which was, for many people, a housing crisis, affecting their ability to pay their rents and exacerbating the problem of damp, uninsulated homes.

As the NHF said in the report: 'It is important to remember that the housing crisis is not one crisis, but a series of interrelated and overlapping crises. These include affordability, the suitability, size and condition of homes, and the ability of people to find accommodation in the first place. Some people will experience one of these problems – others will experience many at once.'

The NHF analysis showed:

- 3.43m people living in overcrowded conditions.
- 2.6m 'concealed homeless' (situations where people need a home of their own but can't get one so are living with family or sofa surfing etc.).
- 2.7m struggling with affordability issues. (The NHF assessed affordability in a number of ways, but, broadly speaking, it took the view that there was an affordability problem if a household's rent or mortgage repayment exceeded 25% of its gross monthly income.)
- 1.36m people in accommodation unsuitable for their needs (for example, needs to do with their health or their age).

- Over 1m people in properties in bad external condition.
- 406,000 people actually homeless.

Overall, the NHF estimated that there were 7.9m people in some form of housing need, of whom 3.8m, the report concluded, would be best served by living in appropriate social housing. (The 7.9m estimate refers to people with at least one form of housing need, to avoid double-counting because so many households have multiple problems.)

Another very comprehensive report also put it bluntly. *Coming Home – tackling the housing crisis together* is the report of the Commission of the Archbishops of Canterbury and York on Housing, Church and Community, which came out in February 2021.[14] 'Is there a housing crisis? In our view, this is undeniable,' the archbishops said.

In addition to the 8m, there must be millions more who are not in crisis, but who have a blight on their future: typically, young, working people, perhaps with children, who are living in private rented accommodation, with a roof over their heads but always worrying they might be evicted. The insecurity and uncertainty that they experience is not good for them or their children. Just as job insecurity makes it hard for people to build a career, housing insecurity makes it hard for people to establish a life.

Not only are we not meeting current housing needs, but the UK is also not planning for the future as a country with a growing population. The ONS, drawing on the 2021 Census, reported that the population of England and Wales grew by 578,000 between 2021 and 2022.[15] This is only a 1% increase, but there is an inevitable pressure on housing because much of the growth is not due to babies being born but to people coming to this country to work and study: net legal immigration to England and Wales from outside the UK was 541,000.

Debate rages around immigration of course, but the interaction between immigration and the housing crisis is not straightforward (for a start, the construction industry building the homes relies heavily on workers from abroad). Asylum seekers have only a marginal impact on the national housing situation. According to the Refugee Council, there are more than 165,000 asylum seekers awaiting an initial decision on their application[16] and, as such, the Home Office has the responsibility to accommodate them, which will typically be in such places as former military bases or the infamous Portland barge, not in council housing. Only if accepted and allowed to stay in the UK can refugees find their own housing. Many will join a local authority waiting list and only receive accommodation depending on priority need, which means the very many asylum seekers who are single men, will not qualify.

So the pressures on housing in the UK continue to grow. Forty years ago, perhaps, policymakers could be forgiven for seeing the rise in owner-occupation since the 1950s and thinking that this would naturally continue, until the vast majority of the population were happy homeowners, leaving a few council rented properties free for those in real economic straits.

But we have to face up to the fact that this is not what has happened. Instead, home ownership is moving further and further out of reach for younger generations and the essential problem is that this country has not put in place any decent alternative to home ownership.

CHAPTER 2

A housing crisis that harms

Social renting – that is, a local authority or housing association tenancy – has dwindled in supply massively over the past 30 years. Some policymakers see that as a sign of progress; I see it as a huge contributory factor to our housing disaster.

According to the housing campaigner, Shelter, since 1991 there has been an average net loss of 24,000 social homes a year.[1] Existing homes are lost to the social rented sector through Right to Buy, plus some get demolished. While there was a significant programme of social housebuilding in the 1990s, this tailed off and never fully filled the gap left by the Right to Buy.

Currently, new build replaces less than half of the missing homes. In 2021-22, figures from the Department for Levelling Up, Housing & Communities show that nearly 25,000 social housing units were sold (because Right to Buy also applies to the homes housing associations took over from councils) and only 7,620 additional social rent units became available.[2]

The result is a deficit in social housing. In England, there are now 1.4m fewer households in social housing than there were in 1980, Shelter reports.

Social housing is not an option available to the many millions of people who can't afford to buy. So where are they living? The answer, of course, is the private rented sector, which has more than doubled since 1980 – from around 2m units to nearer 5m in 2020 according to government figures.[3] This compares to around 4m social housing units.

Private renting mushroomed when banks began to offer Buy to Let mortgages in the early 2000s and many individuals and companies saw renting as a business to be in. Buy to Let now represents around 18% of all current mortgages. The direction of the last 20 years, as house prices became too steep for would-be owner-occupiers, has been a good one for landlords who could come forward with properties to meet demand.

So if the market is meeting the demand for housing, what is the problem? I speak as a landlord myself and I would say that the private rented sector, if managed ethically, is a valuable one. It can provide people with a decent home, in the place they need it, and is often exactly right for their certain circumstances, for example those moving around the country from job to job at the start of their career, people who are not sure of their long-term plans and don't yet want to put down roots, or those who simply don't want the hassle of having to repair and maintain a property. Many young people are happy to rent privately while they save for a deposit to get a mortgage.

The problem is that too many people cannot afford market rents, while for many who can afford it, long-term renting does not give them the security they want.

Furthermore, in a market where demand outstrips supply, there are severe problems caused by the lack of protection for tenants against bad landlord practices. This has at least been recognised in the government's Renters (Reform) Bill, though we have yet to see the legislative plans translated into real action.

Why bad housing matters

This problem of a lack of decent, secure housing for a growing section of the population is deeply serious for this country. The situation has been building up for years, yet politicians and policymakers seem reluctant to acknowledge it, let alone tackle it.

Being badly housed is no longer a problem solely for people on the margins, the poorest in society (though they desperately need help too). It's now a mainstream issue, albeit generational, in that it mainly affects people under 40. It's mainstream in the sense that even people in professional jobs – teachers and nurses – cannot afford to buy a home and in some areas struggle to afford to rent.

Why does this matter, for anyone other than these individuals?

It does matter because the social consequences are far-reaching.

Housing is a major part of most people's cost of living. If rent or mortgage payments were already a stretch for household budgets, the effects of the pandemic, rapid inflation and mortgage interest rate rises in 2022 made them snap.

Inability to afford housing is one of the grievances feeding into strikes by public sector workers – even the better-paid ones. A survey by the British Medical Association (BMA) in December 2022 found that nearly half (45.3%) of junior doctors had struggled to afford their rent or mortgage in the past year.[4] To earn more, some were taking on extra shifts and the BMA said this added to its concerns around junior doctor exhaustion and burnout.

The consequences reach out to the public at large, as housing problems hit staff recruitment in health services, education and so on. The NHS visibly can't cope: basic structures are crumbling.

The consequences are also hitting businesses and the economy, when in some parts of the country people can't afford to live near the jobs they want.

Productivity in the UK is known to be poor in relation to other countries, but academics at the Economics Observatory point out that: 'Research on the reasons for this poor performance has often failed to look at how people's housing costs, locations and living conditions might affect their productivity – for example, through their proximity to jobs that match their skills.'[5]

People can get trapped in a vicious circle: unable to get a tenancy because they haven't got a job, unable to take up a job because they haven't got housing nearby. One of the many evils of zero-hours contracts is the impact they have on a worker's ability to access decent housing, with landlords (not surprisingly) reluctant to take on a tenant who can't demonstrate a regular income.

At the extreme, poor housing is fatal. This was brought home forcefully with the tragedy of the Grenfell Tower fire in 2017, in which 72 people lost their lives. It was a preventable and foreseeable disaster: warnings about the dangers for tower block-dwellers in a fire and the risks of flammable cladding had been made repeatedly for years, most notably after the Lakenal House fire in Camberwell in 2009, which killed six people. Recommendations were made but little was done. Concerns about the flammability of the cladding and poor internal fire protection had been voiced loudly and repeatedly by Grenfell residents, but, again, nothing had been done.

Grenfell was a housing disaster on every level: in the design and structure of the building itself; in the design and procurement of the so-called improvements which turned out to be deadly; and in the management of the property, with the landlord having no meaningful relationship with the tenants.

Housing and the nation's health

We know too that bad housing kills in other ways. The ruling by the coroner in November 2022 that two-year-old Awaab Ishak's death from respiratory problems was directly caused by long exposure to black mould in his family's social housing flat in Rochdale prompted shock and a public recognition that cold, damp and mould can kill. The ruling should be a 'defining moment for the UK's housing sector,' the coroner said, emphasising that this was a housing problem, not just a health problem.

As with Grenfell, there was a familiar history of the Ishak family complaining repeatedly to the landlord, Rochdale Boroughwide Housing, about the mould and being ignored.

Shockingly, it appears the problem is still not being taken seriously enough. An investigation by *The Observer* found that complaints from tenants about disrepair, mould and damp had shot up in the aftermath of the Rochdale tragedy, yet the housing ombudsman investigating the complaints on average imposed a penalty of less than £500 on the social housing landlord.[6]

In the private rented sector too, problems of damp and mould are not being tackled or even acknowledged. *The Observer* reported that councils in England received nearly 24,000 complaints in 2021-22 from private tenants about damp and mould but inspected less than half of these.[7] Even where the inspectors found illegal and dangerous levels of damp and mould, very little formal action was taken: local authorities issued only 1,539 legal orders forcing landlords to make improvements and undertook only 27 prosecutions. Councils blamed budget cuts for the lack of action.

Landlords hate dealing with the problem of mould as there is no easy solution; very often the root cause is the poorly built, uninsulated properties that are typical of this country's housing stock. An estimated 120,000 households in England live in social housing that has problems with condensation and mould, according to official figures, plus a further 176,000 private renting households.[8] The NHS advises that mould can produce allergens, irritants, and toxic substances, and can trigger asthma attacks. Alongside the health dangers, there's the stress for a household of having its bedding, clothes and belongings ruined. Damp and mould problems can only have got worse for many households in the winter of 2022-23, unable to afford to heat their homes properly due to high gas and electricity costs.

The Covid pandemic and its aftermath showed

that the UK has deep-seated health problems, including mental health issues, and poor housing conditions play a part in this. Cold, damp conditions affect even a healthy person and much mental stress is caused by housing issues – not only worries about paying the rent, but also overcrowding, frustration at repairs not getting done, troublesome neighbours and many more problems.

All this is putting pressure on the NHS, as is another consequence of unsatisfactory housing: 'bed blocking' – when elderly or disabled people cannot leave hospital after treatment because their existing home is not suited to their needs.

In January 2023 the NHS reported that 14,000 beds in a week were taken up by people who no longer needed to be there.[9] Typically, these patients cannot be discharged because the social care package for them is not in place, which is partly due to social services being unable to do the work but is also very much to do with housing. All too often these people are living in homes that were already unsuitable for them before they became ill – on the fourth floor of a block of flats with no working lift, too small to accommodate a wheelchair, poorly heated and damp, and so on. Social services can't allow them to go back into those properties, but there is a shortage of well-adapted places for them. The Building Research Establishment has forecast that inappropriate housing for the elderly will cost the country nearly £20bn by 2041 through its impact on health and social services.[10]

At the other end of the generational scale, the impact on children of living in bad and insecure housing is immense, but not easily measured because it can show in numerous ways: poor health; educational underachievement because of stress at home or overcrowding making it difficult to do homework; mental health issues and behavioural issues. When families have to move from one rented place to another, they can't put down roots and create a home; children grow up without that fundamental security and also without social connections, when they can't make friends nearby.

Homelessness horrors

The number of families accepted as homeless by their local authority but placed in temporary accommodation, such as bed and breakfast hotels, because there is no social housing for them, continues to grow. For years this has been recognised as the worst of both worlds: bad for the homeless families and a bad use of council taxpayers' money. But by October 2023 English councils were housing the highest ever number of households in temporary accommodation – 104,000 – at a cost to the taxpayer of £1.7bn a year.[11] In a petition to the government, 119 local authorities asked for help in meeting the cost of temporary accommodation, warning that rising homelessness pressures could tip some councils into bankruptcy[12] (not an empty threat when several councils, including Birmingham City Council, have now gone bankrupt[13]).

Yet all the pressures are there for homelessness to continue to be driven upwards as private sector rents rise, supply falls and evictions increase.

Temporary accommodation means generally the bare minimum – frequently a single hotel room – and is nowhere near temporary enough. Families can be trapped there for years. Research by Shelter published in March 2023 – entitled *Still Living in Limbo* – found that two-thirds of the households in temporary accommodation that they surveyed had no access to their own cooking or laundry facilities and in one third the children did not even have their own bed.[14]

Again – all this has wider consequences for society. Not only are children living in a single room not reaching their potential, but with their health and education suffering they can get trapped in a cycle of poverty and, in the worst cases, go on to offending: Shelter has estimated half of young offenders have experienced homelessness.

Local authority housing waiting lists now sit at over 1.2m households[15] and this is undoubtedly an underestimate of housing need, since the criteria for being accepted onto the waiting list are tight. The figure is down from the peak of 1.85m in 2012 for England but not because there was more housing for them after that date. On the contrary. Instead, the

2011 Localism Act allowed councils to be stricter about whom they allow on to the list, with many then requiring prospective social housing tenants to have a 'local connection' with the area, for instance by having lived there a certain length of time. This eased the pressure on local authorities, which had no possibility of housing the rising numbers on their waiting lists, but it meant hundreds of thousands of households around the country were struck off the lists.

A normal crisis

All these issues are widely known, reported on, studied, campaigned about and worried about, but to a great extent they have also become normalised. It seems that's what the UK is – a society that has been drained by the human and financial cost of housing problems for years but is unwilling to do anything about it.

Are these problems inevitable because much of Britain – certainly much of England – is, after all, a small and crowded place with a growing population and a lacklustre economy?

I believe they are not inevitable, and housing can be better for people. There is no need for millions to be struggling in poor-quality, insecure homes.

Council housing used to be plentiful and sought after, until it was neglected and reduced to 'residual' status, in other words, housing of last resort for people who can't afford anything else, with all the stigma that goes with that.

Home ownership used to be attainable for households earning a reasonable income, as millions of people in their 50s and 60s can testify.

Private renting has never been a favoured option in this country – hence the popularity of home ownership and good quality council housing – but there is no reason why it cannot be a decent, secure and affordable form of housing, as it is in many European countries. In Germany and Switzerland, for example, almost as many people rent privately as own their homes and although there are many reasons for this – financial, legal, cultural – it suggests that one form of housing tenure isn't necessarily 'better' for society than another. What counts is whether people have a decent home where they can enjoy their lives.

We have allowed the housing crisis in the UK to become acute but, as I hope to show in this book, there are ways out of it if we are prepared to change, not only policies, but biases and prejudices about housing that are not serving this country.

CHAPTER 3

Where did housing go wrong?

If our housing disaster is not inevitable, how did we get into such a mess?

We can find the reason in a succession of policy decisions over the past 40 years: some were well-intended, others ideological, and others merely cost-cutting. Problems also grew as a result of inaction as much as action.

Overall, despite the fact that housing is of fundamental importance to the lives of everyone, and to the social and economic wellbeing of the nation, there has been remarkably little vision by political leaders in this area and a distinct lack of long-term thinking. That there have been 15 housing ministers since 2010 only goes to show what a low priority it has been for governments. Housing, which is fundamental to people's lives, is too often overseen by ministers who have little interest in or commitment to the issues but who know that putting in time on this lowly brief is a step on the road to promotion to more 'important' posts.

Such a huge issue as housing deserves more: it is not a minor concern to be delegated to a junior minister. We need real leadership at the top to provide the willpower, funds, and infrastructure to tackle the crisis.

There are three strands to the country's housing problem now: one is that buying a home has become unaffordable for huge swathes of the population; the second is that social housing has declined in numbers to the point that it comes nowhere close to accommodating the people who need it, resulting in long waiting lists, large numbers of people accepted by local authorities as homeless but placed in temporary accommodation and a further problem of hidden homelessness.

Thirdly, the private rented sector, which is currently the only housing tenure open to people who cannot access either home ownership or social housing, is also in crisis. A combination of rising rents, insufficient supply and a legal framework that fails to protect tenants from insecure tenancies, unfair evictions, and unregulated, unsafe conditions, means that hundreds of thousands of people are trapped in bad rented housing. Having said that, this strand is the one where improvements could be made fast, given the political will.

So how did things go so wrong in all three areas?

Why has home ownership become unaffordable?

As people over 50 keep saying – no doubt to the mounting irritation of younger generations – buying your own home didn't use to be an unachievable dream. Owner-occupation rose steadily through the second half of the 20th century because it was very achievable for people earning a regular wage. The ratio of incomes to house prices was such that in the 1950s and 60s, a household with a single earner (typically the man) could afford a family-sized home. Later, two incomes were needed but by then more women were in paid work. Young people were buying flats on their own, particularly as women were helped by the change in the law in the 1970s, which meant they no longer had to have the signature of a man to take out a mortgage.

The idea of the housing ladder took hold: you started with a small flat, or maybe a run-down property that could be done up. You then sold at enough of a profit to buy somewhere bigger. It all seemed perfectly normal and people began to feel it was a law of nature that house prices should rise, steadily and continuously. Even the economic crisis of the early 1990s, when many people found themselves uncomfortably in negative equity, didn't really shake the belief. They sat it out and indeed, house prices did 'recover', as if it had been a nasty but temporary illness.

What people didn't expect was that house prices

would run away from them, the inexorable rise no longer benefiting them but penalising them.

This trend has been happening over the past 20 years, with just a blip caused by the 2008 financial crisis. Up until around 2000, the highest that the multiple of house prices to men's earnings (specifically men's) had reached was a brief peak of prices at six times average earnings in London in the late 1980s boom. Since 2000, the multiple has been rising in every corner of Britain.[1]

In 2021, average house prices stood at 12 times average male earnings in London, and only a little less in the rest of the south-east. As you'd expect – because we're a country in which wealth is concentrated in the south – house prices fall as you get further north but so do earnings. The multiple is around 7.5 times average earnings in the Midlands, while the north-west and Yorkshire, alongside Wales, are on around 6.5 times. Scotland is the most affordable region, with a multiple of 5.5 times average earnings.

Even 5.5 or 6.5 are hardly 'affordable'. For women, whose average earnings are lower, the picture is worse: the average house in London would cost over 14 times the average woman's salary.

These figures are based on average earnings, so of course (certainly outside London) people on better salaries can afford to buy, but more and more cannot.

So how did we get to the position of having a housing market where more or less an entire generation of would-be consumers can't afford the product on sale?

There are numerous, interlocking reasons why this has happened. A well-researched programme produced by the BBC and the Open University (BBC/OU), *Britain's Housing Crisis: What Went Wrong?*, broadcast in October 2023, told the story of what has happened over the past 20 years.[2] What is striking is that the growing problem of excessive house price inflation has been visible all along, and has prompted many a report into what to do about it – yet nothing of significance has ever really been achieved and several of the measures to tackle the affordability issue have made it seriously worse.

The long period of extremely low interest rates (up until the autumn of 2022) is a big factor. In the early 2000s, with mortgages cheap and readily available, more people became able to buy and demand for properties increased. Very quickly, house prices were rising faster than wages.

A different factor is that more and more buyers were using housing as an investment rather than a place to live. These might be large-scale investors wanting to put their money into assets in London, or they might be individuals taking advantage of Buy to Let mortgages in order to become landlords with a portfolio of half a dozen properties. Buy to Let lending rose from £3.9bn in 2000 to £45.7bn in 2007, the BBC/OU programme reported.

In the lending frenzy, mortgages of 100% or

125% were available and people were taking on huge amounts of debt, reassured by the low interest rates and rapidly increasing capital values, both of which would surely go on forever.

But, already, policymakers could see there was a problem as, for the first time in a century, the percentage of households owning their own home began to decline. Britain's steady upward path to being a property-owning democracy had faltered. More and more money was being lent out in mortgages but the loans were fuelling price rises, not creating more homeowners.

Yet the mere fact of house prices rising has always been greeted by politicians and newspaper headlines as unquestionably a good thing (whereas rising wages tend to be deemed a bad thing). At the same time, there has been a long-term trend of house prices in the south – particularly in pretty areas and places with good transport links – being pushed up by people moving out of London, delighted to find that selling even a small property in London allows them to buy an attractive house in a market town or by the sea. Meanwhile, local residents look on with frustration as prices move further out of their reach. This trend has extended out into the Midlands, East Anglia and the south-west as people are prepared to do longer commutes and, in fact, will probably pick up pace now that more professionals work from home at least part of the week.

Is the basic problem one of supply?

Prices go up, of course, when demand rises faster than supply. Even if all other things were equal, the demand for housing in the UK would be rising because not only is the population growing but the number of households is also increasing. According to the Office for National Statistics (ONS), there were an estimated 28.2m households in the UK in 2022, an increase of 6.1% (1.6m) since 2012.[3] This includes families, couples, and single people. In addition, there are many more 'potential' households: ONS analysis of the 2021 census found 4.9m young adults still living with their parents, an increase of 15% on 2011. The figure might be inflated by the fact that the census was taken during the pandemic, but, even so, it points to a lot of people who would probably like to have homes of their own but can't afford it.

Since the Barker report, governments have tended to look on high house prices as a purely supply issue, with the implication that increasing the volume of new homes for sale will solve the problem.

I think this is unrealistic. For years, this idea of increased supply – the fabled 300,000 homes – has been dangled in front of the electorate but has never actually happened. Politicians repeatedly blame 'planning' for this, suggesting that bureaucrats in town halls are holding back the developers who would love to build new homes for all if only they were permitted.

There are indeed a lot of issues with planning, and I'll go into this in more depth in chapter 7, but to put it all on planning is to ignore some very obvious realities.

One is that the big private developers (the eight major housebuilding firms) don't actually want to build many more homes. Over the past 50 years – whatever the planning regime or colour of the government – up to around 250,000 new homes have been built a year and this seems to be an amount developers are comfortable with.

The big housebuilders are very happy with the way things are, as Professor Ian Cole and Research Fellow Tom Archer of Sheffield Hallam University explained to the BBC/OU programme. Their research shows that for the big firms, 'profits before volume' is the model.[4]

'The business model of the housebuilding sector has always been to drip feed new supply. You don't want to move into increasing supply and flooding the market,' Professor Cole told the programme.

'Their strategy is to prioritise margin over volume,' Tom Archer said. 'What that means is that you grow the sale price, you grow the margin, the profit on each home rather than building more housing. You're making your money through price increases rather than through increased output.'

From a business point of view, this has been a successful strategy for the housebuilders. There has been enough demand and enough money circulating in the system to keep prices high, and the big housebuilders and their shareholders have benefited enormously.

Of course, they are in business to make profits, but what I see is a lack of openness about the strategy. Instead, housebuilders and politicians collude in the fiction that they would dearly love to build vastly more housing if only the planning system and NIMBY communities would let them.

Planning is a restriction on building. It is supposed to be, in order to prevent a free-for-all in our crowded country. The system is also there to take into account the effect that new building has on the surrounding community, in terms of road traffic, school places and so on. Sometimes planning decisions seem irrational but they are all part of the democratic process. They can be challenged and frequently are. Yes, there is nimbyism (we all tend to say not in *my* back yard, if we're honest) but, again, this is something a democratic country has to deal with.

Local authorities argue that they are not the ones holding back supply. A Local Government Association (LGA) survey of its members in 2020 found that 2,564,600 units had been granted planning permission by councils since 2009-10 but only 1,530,680 had been completed.[5] Even allowing for the time lag between permission being granted and completion of the build, 1m homes in a decade is a serious shortfall.

The number of planning permissions granted for new homes had almost doubled since 2012-13 with councils approving 9 in 10 applications, the LGA said, arguing that the backlog of unbuilt homes shows the planning system is not a barrier to housebuilding. Instead, it said, councils should be given powers to tackle the housing shortage by being able to compulsorily purchase land where homes remain unbuilt and should be able to charge developers full council tax for every unbuilt development from the point that the original planning permission expires.

The interaction between the planning system and private housing development is not delivering the homes people need, the government's Competition & Markets Authority (CMA) concluded in a report in February 2024 looking into reasons for the undersupply of housing.[6]

'Around 60% of all houses built in 2021 to 2022 were delivered by speculative private development... the country's reliance on this model has seen the gap widen considerably between what the market will deliver and what communities need,' the CMA said.

The CMA concluded that planning is part of the problem: planning decisions can vary widely and be unpredictable and slow, but the undersupply of housing is also due to the limitations of speculative development. 'The evidence shows that private developers produce houses at a rate at which they can be sold without needing to reduce their prices rather than diversifying the types and numbers of homes they build to meet the needs of different communities (for example providing more affordable housing),' it said.

There are other factors that have been pushing up house prices. The cost of building materials and labour is a significant part of the price of a house and inflation here has been high for a number of years, even before the current cost of living surge. The Building Cost Information Service Private Housing Construction Price Index shows this inflation reached 15.3% in 2022, though it has dropped since then.[7] Alongside rising costs are shortages of supply, causing delays, and labour costs in the building industry have gone up 30% since 2015 – a rise blamed on various factors such as the pandemic, Brexit, and lack of training in this country.

In addition, the situation has been made worse by measures that were supposed to alleviate the affordability problem. Perversely, the government's Help to Buy scheme, introduced in 2013, pushed up prices and developers' profits, and ultimately disadvantaged buyers rather than helping them, all at enormous cost to taxpayers.

The scheme allowed first-time buyers to take out an equity loan (up to £120,000 outside London and £240,000 in Greater London), interest-free for the first five years. The idea was that this would help first-time buyers who did not have enough for a deposit and would enable them to get a more affordable 75% mortgage. Take-up was widespread and the scheme became a long-term part of the system, with more than 55,000 households getting a Help to Buy loan in 2020-21.

The Help to Buy equity loan scheme ended in March 2023. The scheme did apparently prompt an increase in new homes being built, but the main beneficiaries were the housebuilders because house prices rose even more steeply after 2013. Many of the buyers who used the scheme must now be struggling, as the rise in interest rates has left them saddled with mortgages they can't afford, plus the repayments on the Help to Buy loans.

The House of Lords Built Environment Committee, which conducted an inquiry into the demand for housing in the UK, concluded in its report in January 2022 that the Help to Buy scheme had simply prompted developers to raise house prices so buyers were paying more for their homes than they would have done had the scheme not existed. 'We find that the Government's Help to Buy scheme, which will have cost taxpayers around £29bn in cash terms by 2023, inflates prices by more than its subsidy value in areas where it is needed the most. This funding would be better spent on increasing housing supply,' the committee's report says.[8]

Imagine how much social housing could have been built with that £29bn. It is a huge sum over a period when public services were cut back every year due to austerity and local authorities were spending more and more on placing homeless people in expensive temporary accommodation because they no longer had the homes to house them in. This funnelling of taxpayers' money to those who don't need it rather than those who do is a disgrace.

CHAPTER 4

The rise of renting

The reasons for the dire state of housing for people who can't afford to buy are not hard to pinpoint. They are mostly the outcome of deliberate policy decisions gradually removing social renting as a possibility available to people on lower incomes and therefore abandoning them to an underregulated private rental market.

The Right to Buy legislation of 1982 changed the country's housing landscape, but in ways its policymakers did not wholly foresee. In itself, there was nothing wrong with giving council house tenants the right to buy their housing at some sort of discounted prices: people had paid their rents for many years and had as much right as anyone else to aspire to own their home, have a stake in their community and an asset to pass on to their children. In many areas, estates were changed for the better as the new owners invested in improving their properties.

The Conservative government's aim was ideological and political – as believers in the primacy of the market, they considered that private ownership was always preferable to public provision, and they trusted that the new homeowners would gravitate towards voting for them as the party that protected the interests of property owners. Yet the ownership bonanza their huge discounts created in the 1980s and 90s didn't lead to the death of renting – in fact, just the opposite.

The grandchildren of the people who bought their council homes in the 1980s are quite likely now to be living in private rented accommodation. The terrible irony is that this could even be a former council property.

In 2017 an investigation by *Inside Housing* magazine found that 40.2% of the housing stock sold by councils under the Right to Buy was now privately rented out, rising to 70.9% in Milton Keynes, the 'right-to-buy-to-let capital' of England.[1] Given the growth in private renting over the past few years, that percentage is now likely to be higher. At the time, *Inside Housing* estimated that the tenants of these properties would be paying more than twice as much in rent as local authority tenants in the same area would be paying.

Meanwhile the 'nicer' former council homes – the inter-war, cottage-style homes with gardens – are now part of the private housing market, selling for hundreds of thousands of pounds.

Some people made a lot of money out of the Right to Buy, but today's generation on low or moderate incomes are paying the price.

In protecting the interests of owners, successive governments ignored the interests of others. It should have been obvious that allowing council houses to be sold depleted the stock of affordable properties to rent, without in any way changing the circumstances of those people who didn't have the means to buy or rent in the private sector. But, seemingly working on the principle that all council housing was bad, the government banned local authorities from investing the proceeds of sales into new social housing. Instead, they were required to use most of the money to pay off debt. People on low incomes had to join an ever-lengthening queue for the council properties left behind.

The emphasis then moved to housing associations, which had been providing affordable rented housing in their own way (often focusing on particular areas or social needs), but which had not been the main housing 'safety net.'

The Housing Act 1988 placed housing associations as the main providers of social housing. Unlike local authorities, they were allowed to borrow on the open market and so invest in building new properties. Many councils transferred their entire housing stock to a housing association or to one specially set up for the purpose, as that was a means to ensure there could be future investment in the stock. Tenants were often wary of voting to change to the new landlord, but they could see it was the only way they would ever get a new bathroom or a leaking roof replaced.

Many housing associations undertook significant development projects. However, if we've ended up with 1.4m fewer households in social housing than there were in 1980, it looks as if housing associations have not managed to fill the gap.

Housing associations have actually been steered away from building social housing. Since 2010, successive governments have placed more and more emphasis on the grant funding to be allocated only for shared ownership housing, not for social rented housing. If housing associations have wanted to build social housing or assisted/supported living schemes for the elderly or vulnerable (which many see as their mission), they have had to fund these entirely from their own surplus. Many schemes are not viable without grant funding while, at the same time, shared ownership (which relies on the household buying their share of the property being able to get a mortgage) is out of reach for many people in housing need.

Given the increase in population (a growing proportion of which are elderly, more vulnerable people), the massive rise in house prices and the number of people on low incomes, can there really be fewer people wanting or needing social housing now than 40 years ago?

Now that the country has less social housing available to rent, the ill effects are widespread, both for individuals and households, and for society in general.

For renters, the financial advantages of getting a social housing tenancy are huge. According to Office for National Statistics (ONS) data for 2022-23, the median monthly private rent between April 2022 and March 2023 was £825 for England – the highest ever recorded. In London, the median monthly rent stood at £1,500.[2] Compare this with the average council house rent of around £388 a month for England.[3] The gap between social and private rents in London is even wider, with an average £475 monthly social rent in the capital. In addition, rent rises are limited in council and housing association properties to 7% a year.

For many people, therefore, social housing is the only one that is actually affordable for them. If they are claiming housing benefit, their options are further restricted as private landlords often won't take on a tenant on housing benefit.

But the shortage of social housing has created inevitable waiting lists. More than 10% of the 1.2m households on English local authorities' waiting lists have been on the list for more than five years. Many of them will be 'waiting' but without a realistic chance of ever getting one of the dwindling number of council homes because other people whose need is greater (for example if they have young children) and who join the list after them will be housed ahead of them.

The 1.2m is not a reliable indication of housing need. Because of the shortage of homes, councils have tended to impose quite restrictive criteria for inclusion on the list. Typically, only people who are local to the area and who are vulnerable or on very low incomes for whatever reason (for example lone parents, people with disabilities) will be eligible. Only people who have been resident in the UK for at least two years can be eligible.

At the same time, the homelessness problem puts additional pressure on local authorities. Under the Housing Act 1996, a person who is homeless or about to become homeless applies to the local authority, which, if it finds they are in priority need and have not intentionally made themselves homeless, has a legal duty to place them and their household in temporary accommodation. 'Priority need' generally means people with dependent children or people who are vulnerable in some way, for example pregnant, fleeing domestic abuse, having a disability, leaving care or having lost a home due to some disaster, like flooding. The reality is that the priority need requirement excludes many people, particularly single men, so even a man leaving prison who has nowhere to go would not be eligible for help from the local authority.

Such is the shortage of council properties now,

this temporary accommodation is more likely to be a bed & breakfast hotel than a council flat (and we'll come to the scandal of temporary accommodation), but if a household is in acute need they might move on to the waiting list ahead of people who are already on the list but whose needs are less urgent.

The combination of diminished stock and restricted eligibility for it has changed the nature of many social housing estates, adding to the misery of the residents and the general view of the outside world that such estates are ghettoes to be shunned. With the best-quality properties taken out by Right to Buy, councils were left with a rump of the worst properties, and an ever-shrinking capital budget to maintain and repair them. Meanwhile, if only the poorest and most vulnerable people are housed, the social mix of an estate changes. Households perpetually on the edge can't create a strong community and are vulnerable to crime moving in. All the worst stereotypes about council estates can become reality if the local authority or housing association does not manage the estate well and fails to take decisive action against anti-social behaviour.

I don't believe social breakdown and crime are inevitable on social housing estates, but the neglect of social housing and its tenants undoubtedly has consequences and it doesn't take long for an estate to slip into a downward spiral.

Is the social housing mess really relevant to the vast majority of people who are not social housing tenants? Why should homeowners care what goes on in council estates?

I would argue that it does matter. In my view, it is an increase in social housing that we need in order to tackle our housing disaster, and we need to do that while not repeating the problems of the past. If we learn the lessons, we can have a real impact on the crisis. I'll explore this further in the next chapter because I believe it is our approach to social housing, for too long the poor relation of housing tenures, that is the way out of the current disaster.

Private renting tensions

Problems with the private rented sector are coming to the fore now, which is not surprising. The sector has had to carry the burden of the country's housing deficiencies, which it has not been designed to do. For years, short-term private renting worked well for certain sections of the population, such as students and young people starting out in jobs. It was not structured to provide long-term housing for families.

A ready supply of Buy to Let mortgages has enabled the private rented sector to balloon in size. In the first quarter of 2022 alone, £8.5bn worth of Buy to Let properties were bought by UK landlords.[4] There are now around 2.7m landlords in the country, though most of these are small-scale businesses, with the average landlord having eight properties in their portfolio.

It is interesting to note how many influential people are landlords. An investigation in May 2023 found that 87 MPs were landlords earning more than £10,000 a year in rental income, 34 of whom were receiving rent from two or more properties.[5] Some years ago, *The Guardian* reported that: 'More than 300 councillors in the 40 boroughs with the largest proportion of private homes for rent own multiple properties. One in seven elected representatives in the areas are landlords, according to declarations of interest.'[6] This is not a surprise, given that councillors are often drawn from the business community, but it does create potential conflicts of interest when the local authority is also supposed to be regulating and inspecting private rentals. Legally, councillors have to declare their interests and not vote on matters in which they have an interest.

When mortgage interest rates rose in 2022, the cracks in the inflated rentals sector quickly began to show. Small-scale landlords with no financial reserves had no money for maintaining the properties and tried to pass their mortgage repayment costs on to tenants.

Even before the interest rate rises, high demand for private renting not only pushed up rents but enabled unscrupulous landlords to treat tenants unfairly, making use of section 21 (s21) of the 1988 Housing Act, which allowed them to evict tenants with two months' notice and no need to give a reason. These so-called 'no fault' evictions (meaning the tenants have done nothing wrong) have been used by bad landlords to turf out tenants who complained about damp or disrepair (hence often being called 'revenge evictions'), or to get new tenants in at a higher rent.

While these unfair evictions have hit the headlines, the government has known about them for a long time: in fact, 'eviction after tenants complained to the landlords about disrepair' is one of the categories listed in government statistics showing the reasons for people becoming homeless.[7]

It is good news that the Renters (Reform) Bill, currently passing through Parliament, will abolish s21 and require landlords to prove a legitimate reason for eviction. Housing Secretary Michael Gove has stated that s21 will be abolished in law in 2024. However, there are doubts about when it will be abolished in practice. In a response to the *Select Committee Report on Reforming the Private Rented Sector* in October 2023, the government said: 'Implementation of the new system [for evictions] will not take place until we judge sufficient progress has been made to improve the courts. This means we will not proceed with the abolition of section 21 until reforms to the justice system are in place.' These reforms are due to include 'a new digital system for possessions' but such a system hasn't even been designed yet![8]

Local authorities are suspicious that the justice system reforms are an excuse for doing nothing. 'It is imperative that there is no delay in ending section 21 eviction notices,' the Local Government Association has said. 'Without a sufficient strategy and timescales to address the alleged backlogs, this delay could be indefinite.'[9]

Unfortunately, announcing the abolition of s21 could very well be making things worse for tenants, as unscrupulous landlords are making ever greater use of s21 evictions while they are still legal. Ministry of Justice figures show that in the second quarter of 2023 (after the announcement of the s21 reforms), 8,399 landlords started s21 eviction court proceedings against their tenants. This is the highest number for seven years.[10] A rise in s21 evictions means a rise in homelessness. According to Shelter, government homelessness statistics show that no fault evictions resulted in 24,260 households being threatened with homelessness in 2022-23 – up by 23% compared to the previous 12 months.

The bricks and mortar issue

These factors in our housing disaster are all about people but there is another element: the housing stock itself, which has innumerable problems across all tenures.

The design flaws and structural problems of council estates built in the 1960s and 1970s are well known. Many estates were in such a bad way structurally that they had to be knocked down. On the whole, lessons were learned when it came to building successive social housing properties.

But just because a property is owner-occupied, doesn't mean it is well built. The UK, especially in the major cities, has a high proportion of homes that are more than 100 years old and even newer houses tend to be poorly insulated and hard to heat, as people found to their cost during the winter of 2022-23. Up until the 1980s, building regulations made little requirement for insulation and energy efficiency was barely mentioned.

The government publishes an annual English Housing Survey[11] which looks at, among other things, whether dwellings meet a statutory 'decent homes standard' – whether they are in a reasonable state of repair, safe and reasonably warm. In 2021, 3.4m homes failed to meet this (not very exacting) standard. Social rented homes are required by law to meet this standard but, even so, 10% do not.

In the private sector, 23% of privately rented dwellings failed to meet the decent homes standard, and 13% of owner-occupied properties. A measure has been added to the Renters (Reform) Bill to require private rented homes to meet the decent homes standard. This move is not before time, as the lack of inspection of the private rented sector, plus the threat of eviction if tenants complain about disrepair and damp, has allowed some truly squalid conditions to exist in private rentals.

The bricks and mortar condition of housing in the UK is an important part of the whole picture.

Homes are crucial to the issues we face in the future (in fact, already face) caused by the climate crisis and environmental crisis. Construction work, and the properties themselves, have a huge impact on energy use, on the natural environment and on the urban environment – the way people live their lives. In the 20th century, energy efficiency, pollution and environmental issues were not much taken into account when planning and building housing. That is changing and in the future there is no excuse for not putting these considerations centre stage.

In the next chapters I'll look in more depth at the different housing sectors and what I think needs to be done.

CHAPTER 5

The shrinking of social housing

An objective look at the problems I've outlined in the previous chapters would immediately identify the key issue: decent housing on long-term secure tenancies let at rents people can genuinely afford is the big glaring gap in our housing provision. That kind of secure tenancy can only be had in social housing and the UK does not have enough of it, whether provided by local authorities or housing associations.

Incomes are failing to keep pace with the cost of living, illness and vulnerability are rising as an ageing population struggles to cope with the aftermath of the pandemic, and workers are frequently unable to buy a home in the area they live in. Doesn't it seem obvious that social housing is what's needed here to get the country back on its feet?

However, we rarely look at the issues with clear vision as, in the UK, we seem to have been conditioned to think that social housing is a problem, not a solution. It is very difficult to have a rational conversation about social housing without the talk blundering into the usual stereotypes of crime-ridden estates filled with single mothers on benefits and marauding teenagers. This is not to deny that severe social problems exist in certain places, but the causes are far more to do with economic factors than actual bricks and mortar. Yet, over the years, government policies have reduced the number of homes available, as if this in itself would make the social problems go away.

My argument is that to tackle our housing disaster, the extra supply we need is, essentially, social rented homes and to do this properly, in a way that learns from the mistakes of the past, we need to move away from warped views of the sector.

We have to face the facts, drop fantasies that we will ever reach a nirvana of home ownership for all and acknowledge that millions of people need homes that are developed in such a way – proactively by the state – that residents can have tenancies at rents they can realistically afford and which will not increase beyond their means. If people are unwaged and reliant on benefits, their rents should be at such a level that they can be fully covered by housing benefit (which is not the case now in many areas). So, provided people pay their rents and don't indulge in anti-social behaviour, they can create a home secure in the knowledge they won't be evicted.

Once we're able to talk about this without prejudice against social housing and the people who live in it, we can get down to the task of working out how to provide it.

Why has this country turned against social housing? Undoubtedly, the sector has an unfavourable reputation among people who don't live in it (though not necessarily among those who do).

It is worth looking back at social housing, both in the 20th century and more recently, to see what it achieved and where it went wrong – considering that some of the bad outcomes were the result of well-intentioned experiments and some were down to deliberately punitive policies.

A history of ups and downs

The story of social housing is well told in John Boughton's carefully researched book *Municipal Dreams: The Rise and Fall of Council Housing.*[1]

Boughton relates how the combination of wartime bombing, which had destroyed huge swathes of housing in London and other cities, plus a recognition that it was no longer acceptable to have people living in overcrowded slum conditions, with no bathroom or inside toilet, prompted the state to embark on ambitious building programmes in the 1950s. Local authorities vied with each other to build the most homes. Progressively minded architects aimed to design estates that would give people better lives: not just the basics of inside toilets but 'streets in the sky' to replace the bombed streets on the ground, windows designed to maximise sunlight, green space for children to play in (with kitchen windows facing the green space so that mothers could watch the children), communal laundry rooms and so on. Some of these ideas were good, others didn't last (washing machines in the home replaced laundry rooms), but the guiding principle was that people should enjoy living in these homes and, to begin with, they certainly did.

The idea of providing housing for the poor goes back to the 19th century, with charitable housing providers such as the Peabody Trust (and perhaps even further back, with traditional almshouses for the elderly poor), but Labour's 1949 Housing Act did not envisage the new social housing as intended only for low-income families. Minister for health and housing, the legendary Nye Bevan, wanted 'the most variegated kind of housing' and was very opposed to 'segregation of the different income groups'. He argued that mixed communities would be stronger, so the housing built by councils was to be 'general needs' housing.

Boughton shows how the question of whether social housing should be for anyone, or whether it should be restricted to those on low incomes – in other words part of the welfare system – went back and forth over the decades until what we have now is effectively housing for the most deprived, and not even meeting that need well.

More than 800,000 council homes were built under Labour between 1945 and 1951. The subsequent Conservative government continued the job, with 229,000 council homes in 1953, the most ever built in one year. Some of these were high-rise estates, which were starting to be constructed in the major cities.

However, the Conservatives wanted to promote owner-occupation 'by all possible means' and required local authorities to move more towards regenerating slum areas as their primary housing activity.

The building of new housing by local authorities tailed off from that point and policy shifted towards council housing being treated as housing only for the poor. This might seem sensible, John Boughton says, 'but it contains a dangerous logic which has reached its conclusion at the present time. When council housing is seen as housing of last resort – a safety net for the poorest or most vulnerable, even in present terms a temporary safety net – it (and its residents) are seen as second rate.'

'Residualisation', Boughton explains, is the term for this process of council housing becoming housing only for the most needy. Successive governments have viewed social housing in this way – housing for people who can't afford anything else. This means people end up in a dispiriting competition as to 'who is the neediest' in order to get access to the rapidly drying up pool of homes.

I would argue that we need an end to the mindset that social housing must be residual housing if we are to tackle this country's problems.

An unfortunate result of the boom years of council house building was that the actual construction of the properties became a problem in itself. Getting people out of the slums was a big priority in cities in the 1960s and ambitious high-rise estates were designed, constructed with new system-building techniques. But the Ronan Point disaster of 1968 exposed all the dangerous flaws of this approach: an accidental gas explosion on the 18th floor of the Ronan Point tower block in Newham brought down one whole corner of the block like a collapsing house of cards and four people were killed. Investigations uncovered how badly built and structurally unsound the block was (and others like it).

In the 1970s, certain estates went rapidly downhill: construction flaws became evident while basic problems, like lifts not working, became an everyday nuisance for residents. There's been much analysis of what went wrong with the design and building of these estates and the upshot for many of them was that the tower blocks were pulled down and replaced with low-rise housing. The design and construction flaws were not the fault of the people who lived there but, mixed with the social problems of poverty and crime, they added to the stigma attached to council estates.

Right now, I think we have to combat that stigma if the country is to get the housing it needs. Plenty of well-designed and lasting developments were built, and for the future we can learn as much from what did work as from what didn't.

Something that had a significant effect on social housing was Labour's 1977 Housing (Homeless Persons) Act, which placed a statutory duty on local authorities to house people in priority need – principally pregnant women and families with dependent children, or people with health or disability issues. The policy itself was well-intentioned, as there's no doubt people in these groups urgently need housing, but, over time, as the Right to Buy ate into the stock of council homes, the consequence was that only people deemed vulnerable could get a council house. At one time, a young couple could have put their names on the waiting list in the reasonable hope of getting a home in which to start a family – that became no longer an option.

At the same time, where there is scarcity there is competition and allegations of 'cheating'. Certain groups of people get accused of 'jumping the queue', even though they may be in genuine priority need.

Another strand of the housing crisis became apparent at this time: the growing dependency of tenants on housing benefit, with the consequent increase in the state's welfare bill. Council tenants were increasingly likely to be on very low incomes, unemployed, sick, or to be lone parents. More and more claimed rent rebates, or housing benefit as it is now called. John Boughton reports that overall local government expenditure on housing benefit rose from £841m in 1980-81 to £3.35bn ten years later.

Between 1980 and 1990, while the council housing stock dwindled as a result of the Right to Buy, the annual number of households accepted as homeless by local authorities rose by more than 100,000 – from 76,342 to 178,867.

People accepted as homeless tended to be placed in a council's most hard-to-let properties, creating a downward spiral of unpleasant and unpopular dwellings lived in by people who were poor, unemployed, or (increasingly, with the advent of care in the community) had mental health problems. Pretty soon, some estates gained a bad reputation and no-one else wanted to live there.

The statutory duty to house the people in the priority groups who are homeless still applies, but councils now no longer have the homes to give them, which is why they get placed in temporary accommodation and we have the scandal of families living in a single hotel room.

The Right to Buy and its consequences

As we know, Margaret Thatcher's government changed social housing radically when the 1980 Housing Act gave people who had been council tenants for more than three years the right to buy their homes at a substantial discount. In 1984 the qualifying period was lowered to two years and the maximum discount raised to 60%.

Council tenants knew a good deal when they saw it and by 1997 more than 1.8m council homes had been sold – about 25% of the total stock. Of course, these were likely to be the nicest homes – particularly 'cottage-style' houses with gardens – on the most settled and least troubled estates. High-rise flats were less popular, though many have sold.

Local authorities were required to give most of the proceeds to the Treasury rather than reinvest them in new housing. The result was soon evident; Boughton notes that in 1978-79, more than 79,000 new council homes were started in England and Wales; by 1996-97 the figure had fallen to 400 new builds. This was welcomed by policymakers who believed in the supremacy of the market: in their view, rented council housing was not subject to the market and was therefore bad for society and bad for those who lived in it.

The Right to Buy was definitely good for those who could take advantage of it and it brought millions of people into home ownership who would not otherwise have been able to afford it. They bought the homes they loved and put their stamp on them; it was said it was easy to spot the RTB homes on an estate as they had new front doors.

But the Right to Buy was also divisive and did a real disservice to those tenants who could not afford, or simply didn't want, to buy. There was a social polarisation, as poorer tenants got placed, and then were stuck, on poorer estates. 'Poorer' not only in terms of income but in terms of quality of life and quality of the actual buildings as local authorities had less money to maintain them: annual government subsidy to councils for building and maintenance was cut by nearly half during the 1980s.

The big problem with Right to Buy is that not only does it deplete the social housing stock, but it is a major disincentive to providing more social rent homes. Why should councils and housing associations invest in building homes, if those properties are going to be out of their stock and into private hands within a few years?

Homes England, the government's housing and regeneration agency, calls for community bodies, investors, and developers to be 'Investment Partners' and bid for funding under the Affordable Homes Programme. This is something ethical investors would be interested in, where they see a need for building new social housing. Yet properties built with funding from Homes England are subject to the statutory Right to Acquire, which allows eligible tenants to purchase their homes at a discount.[2] It is the Right to Buy under another name and it is a major deterrent to ethical investors who want to increase the supply of social housing. They do not want to waste their money by having those homes disappear into private ownership after only a few years.

Enter the housing associations

To talk of 'council housing' now is a little misleading as, in the 1990s, housing associations began to take on the role of major provider of social rented housing. Many 'council estates' are actually housing association estates with a mix of privately owned homes bought under the Right to Buy, within them.

In the 1990s, under the Conservatives and then Labour, the idea grew that the trouble with council housing was that it was *council* housing, and estates would be improved if the landlords were housing associations, which would bring in capital investment from private sector partners.

John Boughton's book traces the bewildering succession of initiatives from both Conservative and Labour governments – Housing Action Trusts, Estate Action, New Deal for Communities, to name but a few – all launched by gung-ho housing ministers and all intended to 'solve' the problem of council housing by changing the design of the buildings, or the financing and ownership of the stock, or the social mix of the residents. All too often, the solution to a 'problem' estate seemed to be to get rid of the existing residents. Boughton quotes many dispiriting examples of estates where residents who voted for a new scheme, in the hope of getting the necessary repairs and modernisation done to their homes, were decanted out while works were completed, but were then never allowed back. Many regeneration schemes were financed by part of the land or the resulting new-build housing being sold off at market prices, so the net amount of social housing was less than it was before. The social mix of the estate was then deemed to be 'improved'.

Boughton points to a kind of 'state-led gentrification' as he calls it, particularly happening in London, where estates are regenerated in partnership with private developers and end up with a fraction of the number of council homes they formerly had.

One of the most extreme examples is Balfron Tower in Poplar, east London, designed in the 1960s by the famous architect, Erno Goldfinger, who believed strongly in creating good housing for working people. The modernist building was admired at first, but after a while came to be considered one of the worst examples of ugly council tower blocks. However, emptied of council tenants and refurbished, its flats were then marketed as glossy and fashionable homes for City workers, with prices starting at around £375,000 for a one-bedroom flat, plus a hefty service charge. The promotional website gushed that 'Erno Goldfinger's vision for Balfron Tower was to focus on the community.' After 'a careful restoration of a design icon,' the website said, 'we have created a collection of distinctive interiors that make the most of the generous interior space, and incredible views across east, south and west London.' There was no mention of the fact that the lovely space and views were once enjoyed by Tower Hamlets council tenants before they were decanted. The ironic twist to this story is that the marketing was halted in 2023, the developers apparently at that point having failed to sell a single flat, and the future use of the building remains to be seen.[3]

The process of local authority-built estates only being improved if they were taken over by housing associations, which could bring in private capital, increased rapidly in the first decades of the 21st century. One local authority after another asked its tenants to agree to a large-scale voluntary transfer (LSVT) in which the council's whole housing stock would be transferred to a housing association, either an existing one or one set up for the purpose. Tenants usually voted 'yes' as there were clear short-term advantages for them (and they retained the Right to Buy) – the longer-term uncertainty being how much rents would rise.

The duty to house homeless and vulnerable people remains with the local authority, so what happens in practice is that people on the council waiting list are waiting for housing association homes.

As a result, in 2008, housing associations overtook local authorities as the main social housing providers in England, managing 2m homes compared with local authorities' 1.9m. As of 2021 housing associations were managing 2.5m social homes in England compared with local authorities' 1.6m, according to Office for National Statistics (ONS) data.[4]

Those ONS figures show the total number of social rented homes didn't go up much in that period – only 200,000, from 3.9m to 4.1m. So the move to housing associations as the main provider has not improved supply and has made little difference to the households on local authority waiting lists.

As a demonstration of the housing situation in England, the figures also show that the number of owner-occupied homes rose only slightly, from 15.07m to 15.86m, during those 13 years, while the most significant increase was in the number of private rented homes, which went up from 3.4m to 4.9m and overtook the total of social rented homes in England.

The regeneration roundabout

An alternative to an LSVT was another acronym, the ALMO – an arm's length management organisation. This is a non-profit-making organisation wholly owned by the local authority. The council still owns the housing stock but the ALMO manages it. When this model was brought in in the early 2000s, the incentive was that only a council that set up an ALMO could have access to capital investment. Later, some of these were transformed into housing associations.

Some council estates were regenerated under Private Finance Initiative (PFI) arrangements – the kind of complex financial deals that have become notorious for saddling hospitals with heavy debt and are blamed for the catastrophic reduction in NHS hospital beds.

Several local authorities also discovered the downside of PFI. In 2022 the London Borough of Islington brought the management of more than 4,000 social homes back in-house after a 16-year PFI contract ended. Tenants had been very unhappy about the management and there had been accusations of public money being siphoned off to offshore accounts.[5]

As a result of all these initiatives, there is a vast array of different ways of providing social housing, both between local authorities and within them. One social housing estate might be owned and managed very differently from another nearby, which might look very similar. Many have been regenerated via complex and opaque financial deals, which, in the long run, will have been poor value for taxpayers' money.

Many of the 'regeneration' schemes have been convoluted ways for the state *not* to invest in social housing, but to pass the buck onto private capital – which, not surprisingly, wants a return for its buck.

Whether any of this has improved life for the residents is another matter – sometimes it has, sometimes it hasn't. Sometimes the private money brought in was used to raise the housing stock to the Decent Homes Standard, which was introduced in 2000. Social landlords were given 10 years to bring their stock up to scratch, which, by and large, they achieved. To meet the standard, homes have to be in a reasonable state of repair, have noise and thermal insulation, an adequately-sized kitchen less than 20 years old and a bathroom less than 30 years old. These common-sense improvements were badly needed: more than 1.5m social rented homes did not meet the standard in 2000.

There is now a crackdown on bad conditions in social housing, with the introduction of the Social Housing (Regulation) Act 2023, also known as 'Awaab's law', which forces social landlords to fix damp and mould problems. As ever, it remains to be seen what effect this will have, but gaps in the law have already become evident. *The Guardian* reported in January 2024 that accommodation for asylum seekers will not be covered by the legislation as it is not technically social housing. Yet refugee charities frequently report that asylum seekers are housed in the cheapest and poorest-quality accommodation, where problems of damp and cold are rife.[6]

In recent years, policy on social housing has been less concerned with the buildings – their design and construction – and has focused more on the residents, their incomes and status. The government's attempts to reduce the ballooning housing benefit bill has hit tenants hard.

The bedroom tax, introduced in 2012, has been a real blow to social housing tenants who receive universal credit or housing benefit. They face a substantial cut in benefit if they are deemed to have more bedrooms than they 'need' – a 14% cut if they have one 'surplus' bedroom and a 25% cut for two or more bedrooms.

The thinking behind this was reasonable: freeing up properties by getting tenants to downsize, for instance if they were in a three-bedroom place but their children had grown up and moved out. However, in practice, local social housing availability is so limited (especially the smaller one- and two-bedroom properties) that few households could downsize even if they wanted to and, instead, they have had to find the extra money to cover the gap in rent.

The bedroom tax has been nothing but punitive for social housing tenants and is widely seen as an unfair imposition on people on low incomes.

The importance of management

I've been talking here mainly about the supply of social housing and why we have ended up with so few homes to let at social rents, but it's important to note that if more social housing is to be provided, it also needs to be managed well.

I'm not shutting my eyes to the fact that social landlords have to deal with a wide range of problems and that, at the extreme, serious anti-social behaviour can be a blight on estates (particularly affecting those residents who are vulnerable).

In 2013 I founded ASB Help, a pioneering charity which gives help and advice to thousands of people every week who are victims of anti-social behaviour.[7] The organisation is now recognised as a national leader in this field, provides training to local authorities, police forces and housing providers, and is a member of the Home Office task force for implementing the government's new anti-social behaviour action plan. Too often, victims don't know where to turn, so the ASB Help website advises them on their rights and equips them with the tools they need to make a complaint to the authorities and get action. To remind us that anti-social behaviour is not a trivial problem, the website is dedicated to the memory of Fiona Pilkington from Leicester, who, in 2007, killed herself and her 18-year-old disabled daughter, Francecca, after Leicester police failed to investigate her 33 complaints to them about harassment.

While anti-social behaviour is not confined to social housing estates of course – far from it – it is one of the problems social landlords frequently have to deal with.

But I have seen with my own eyes that social housing can be good housing. Between 1998 and 2005 I was involved with Irwell Valley Housing Association, which has homes in Greater Manchester, including some areas of real deprivation. I chaired the Gold Service tenants' panel, set up by Irwell Valley HA's then chief executive, the late Dr Tom Manion.

Tom Manion and I shared views on the importance of customer care and Tom came up with many ideas on how to implement this in the world of social housing.[8] In his book *The Reward Society*, he points out the imbalance between landlord and tenant in social housing: the landlord has big responsibilities to maintain and manage the housing, and this is as it should be, but the tenant has little legal responsibility to do anything other than pay the rent. The landlord has few tools to deal with the bad tenants – the ones who get into persistent arrears, trash their homes and make life miserable for their neighbours.

So his approach, with Gold Service, was to address management problems via carrot and stick, reward as well as penalties. As I have shown in my approach to managing my retail business, and, as he sets out in his book, more can be achieved by rewarding good behaviour than by punishing bad.

To make this work, rules have to be firm and well-communicated, so that everyone knows that if you break the rules there will be consequences. If certain tenants don't pay their rent and get away with it, why should others pay dutifully?

Back in 1998, 60% of Irwell Valley's tenants were in arrears at some point. Tom Manion believed that what needed to change was behaviour. He wrote in his book: 'Could we motivate people to improve their behaviour without threatening to take away their home? We asked a simple, radical and important question: why do we treat all our customers the same? Why were we giving our best customers, those who paid their rent on time and looked after their homes, the same service as our worst customers?'

Residents could join the Gold Service scheme if they paid their rent on time and didn't break any other terms of their tenancy agreement. If they got into difficulties paying the rent, they could make an arrangement with Irwell Valley Housing Association to pay off the arrears over a certain period and could rejoin the scheme when the arrears were cleared. There was a range of rewards: in particular, Gold Service tenants got a faster repairs service. That was the carrot, and the stick was fast and firm action against persistent non-payment of rent and anti-social behaviour. During my time with the tenants' panel, I could see the approach working: over a decade it went from only 40% of Irwell Valley tenants qualifying for the scheme to 91% being members – in other words, 91% paying their rent on time.

So I'm aware that building new social housing is not the end of the matter. For rented housing to be good the landlord needs to be good. But good practice is out there already: there are a host of examples of effective and imaginative management by social landlords all over the UK and most of them take their job very seriously. Most would like to supply more homes and some are finding ways of doing that.

In 2018, Theresa May's government removed the 'borrowing cap' which had been in place since 2012. The cap had put a very strict limit on how much local authorities were allowed to borrow within their housing revenue account (the ringfenced part of their budget designated solely for housing) and had severely restricted how much councils could invest in new homes. Those councils that still owned their stock welcomed the lifting of the cap, but the existence of the Right to Buy still means they could be spending money building homes that only a few years later have to be sold at a discount, often at a price below their build cost!

If we are to build more social housing, as I believe we must, the Right to Buy cannot be allowed to eat away at that provision. It is no good building homes for rent but then allowing them to be treated as a step on the ladder to home ownership by selling them at a huge discount, so that individuals profit at the expense of the taxpayer.

My argument is that if we look at social housing objectively, we can see that it has within it the seeds of solutions to our housing disaster. But we have to learn from the decades of meddling and failed policies, stop treating it as 'housing of last resort' and allow it, and its residents, to take their place in the mainstream.

CHAPTER 6

Underregulated and oversubscribed

The private rented sector has grown over the past 20 years to become the second largest housing sector, after home ownership – yet until recently it has been largely ignored by policymakers. The whole sector is now shot through with problems of low standards, unfairness, and unaffordability. As tenants' campaign group Generation Rent says: 'No significant reform of tenure law has taken place in England since the 1980s and 11m private renters live in a sector that is not fit for purpose.'

I do believe that good landlords have an important role to play in housing provision and that they should be allowed to fulfil that role, but the private rented sector, at the moment, is expected to do the impossible.

Private renting is currently not a good substitute for home ownership for households who want to put down roots, and it is not a good substitute for social housing for people on very low incomes. Yet, currently, millions of people can only turn to private renting for a home and, with demand far outstripping supply, the field is wide open for unscrupulous landlords to take advantage.

The Renters (Reform) Bill[1] does at least promise to get rid of the worst abuses by landlords.

Broadly, the Bill proposes to, among other things:

- Abolish section 21 (s21) 'no fault' evictions and move to a simpler tenancy structure.
- Introduce more comprehensive possession grounds so landlords can still recover their property (including where they wish to sell their property) and to make it easier to repossess properties where tenants are at fault, for example in cases of anti-social behaviour and repeat rent arrears.
- Provide stronger protections against backdoor eviction by ensuring tenants are able to appeal against excessively above-market rents designed to force them out. An independent tribunal will be able to determine the actual market rent of a property.
- Introduce a new Private Rented Sector Ombudsman.
- Create a Privately Rented Property Portal to help landlords understand their legal obligations and demonstrate compliance.

These could be useful steps towards improvements though, as I noted in chapter 4, doubts have already arisen as to when the abolition of s21 evictions will actually happen.

Even if a fairer regime is introduced, two decades of rapid expansion of private renting, with little enforcement of standards or protection for tenants, has really shown the limitations of this sector. If it can be brought up to standard, private renting is an important part of the housing mix, but it is currently not the tenure that can carry the responsibility of improving this country's housing on the scale we need.

Given that social renting and home ownership are both out of reach to large swathes of the population, private renting has become the only option for many households. What used to be a sector for students and young people wanting flexibility has become the tenure where people are trying to create a home and raise a family. A large proportion of these people are unhappy with private renting for a host of reasons, ranging from the frustrating – for example, not being able to decorate their homes as they wish – to the deadly serious, where their home is unsafe and threatening their health through mould and damp. Yet, with demand outstripping supply, tenants have little choice or bargaining power and find it difficult to fight back against excessively high rents or landlord abuses.

For two decades, banks have been keen to give

out Buy to Let mortgages at low interest rates, so becoming a landlord has been a canny financial move for those who had the funds. But we should also ask the question of whether this process of more people becoming landlords and more becoming tenants has fed the growing inequality in this country. Buy to Let has surely added to the unaffordability of house prices. Who has the money to buy the £250,000 starter home on a new estate? In the promotional pictures it will be a beaming couple with a child. In practice, the buyer is quite likely to be a landlord buying it to rent out, rather than the young family who will move into it as tenants. People on higher incomes have had the ability and the incentive to become landlords: those on lower incomes rent.

Most private rented tenancies at the moment are assured shorthold tenancies – ASTs. These were introduced in 1989 as a tenancy operating for an agreed period, usually 12 months followed by a review: the idea was to give landlord and tenant both greater flexibility and greater certainty. Both would know how long the tenancy was for and neither would be tied into long, or even open-ended, tenancies. ASTs can be for short periods – six months or even three – or longer, up to three years. Tenancies of more than three years, however, require a much more complex contract, known as a deed, which is a deterrent to long tenancy agreements.

In the 1990s the advent of ASTs did the trick of making private renting easier for both parties and opening up the market. Landlords no longer had the fear of being stuck with tenants on fixed, very low rents and so more homes became available for rent.

However, one person's flexibility is another person's insecurity. Short tenancies of 12 months or less are fine for young working people moving around as they start their career; they are not good for families wanting to put down roots – yet this is the demographic finding themselves more and more confined to private renting. As the demand for tenancies has increased, insecurity for renters has got worse as unscrupulous landlords have not hesitated to use s21 notices to evict people for no reason, safe in the knowledge they can always find other tenants.

It is shocking the extent to which s21 notices have been used as a weapon against tenants who complain about rent increases or about disrepair or danger in their homes. What is particularly insidious is that bad landlords have been doing this to avoid bringing their properties up to scratch. It has been more profitable for them to get rid of the tenants than to do the repairs because they know there is always someone else to rent the sub-standard property. Even if legislation protects tenants from no-fault evictions, the problem of poor-quality housing remains.

For the future, the government says it will legislate to require private rented properties to be brought up to the Decent Homes Standards. Legislation would also give local authorities greater enforcement powers to ensure compliance. If enforced, these further measures would be very significant – but right now, it's a big 'if'.

I would argue that, while it is good to prevent landlords evicting well-behaved tenants at short notice, more needs to be done to give tenants security. It is hard to plan your life around 12- or six-month tenancies. Having to move frequently is highly stressful, and potentially disruptive to children's schooling. In my view, good, professional landlords should be able to offer ASTs of up to five years, if both parties agree, with rent rises pegged to the rate of inflation. Needless to say, the tenancy would still be dependent on timely rent payment and appropriate behaviour.

A responsible landlords' charter

I'm a landlord myself: I aim to act ethically in my dealings with my properties and with tenants, and I'm sure there are many landlords out there who do the same. It could be years before the current government reforms take effect, but there is nothing to stop responsible landlords getting together and signing up to some form of responsible landlords' charter and accreditation scheme, which would have higher standards than the minimum set out by the law as it stands.

I have set up several non-government organisations to raise standards in areas where I felt something needed to be done and it seemed the government was not likely to act quickly enough. A responsible landlords' charter could work on the same lines as the Good Business Charter, which I initiated in 2020.[2] This has been very successful, working with the TUC, the Institute of Directors, the Confederation of British Industry, and the Federation of Small Businesses, to raise ethical standards in businesses. We are attracting new companies all the time to sign up to the Charter's 10 principles of responsible business behaviour, over and above the statutory minimums. This accreditation then acts as a brilliant signpost for consumers who want to support responsible organisations.

The principles of a responsible landlords' charter would be:

- No revenge evictions. If a tenant reports a problem, check it out and, if the problem is genuine, fix it without delay. Your tenants and their children should not be exposed to hazards. Your property is your asset, which needs to be maintained, so treating damp, ensuring that electricals, plumbing and so on are safe and functional – these are not costly burdens but an investment in the property.
- Allow inspections. A responsible landlord won't object to checks by the local authority or a credible third party. Being a landlord is a business and a good business is open to scrutiny.

- It is perfectly reasonable to part company with tenants who don't pay their rent, or who don't act responsibly and honestly towards you as landlord and towards their neighbours. But, other than in those circumstances, evictions should be avoided. It's a huge thing to take someone's home away from them, especially in the current housing shortage.
- Following on from that, I really believe that a landlord and tenant, as willing seller and willing buyer, should agree on the length of the tenancy, which should then be reasonably upheld. As landlord, you might only want to offer a short tenancy if you envisage taking the property back for yourself, or to redevelop it or sell it in the near future. But if you are renting properties as a long-term business, allow people longer tenancies. It's terribly difficult for people to plan their lives, particularly families with kids going through local schools, on one-year tenancies. If someone says, I need a three-year or even a five-year tenancy, as long as they pay their rent and don't display anti-social behaviour, the landlord should allow that longer-term arrangement.
- On a longer-term tenancy, the rent increase will inevitably be an issue. I would propose linking the increase to the RPI (or another index both parties are comfortable with).

Then both parties know what to expect at rent review time.

- A responsible landlord needs to be supportive if a good tenant runs into financial problems. If someone who has paid the rent regularly comes to you and says they've lost their job and can't pay the next month's rent, take a balanced view. It's far better to talk things through and come to a realistic arrangement than to immediately reach for the eviction notice. Recognise that getting another job will take time, or indeed claiming benefit will also take time as there is typically a six-to-eight-week delay before payment. A good landlord should be able to accommodate this gap in payments and agree a plan for the tenant to make up the arrears.
- This approach of course rests on the tenant being open and honest about the situation and keeping to their commitment to pay back the outstanding rent. A good relationship with the tenant needs to have been set up from the start of the tenancy, ideally with a clear explanation of what can be done in a situation of financial difficulties. This is much better than the tenant avoiding telling you of the problem and arrears getting out of control.

A lot of what I'm saying here essentially comes down to fairness. The Fairness Foundation, also a charity I've founded, which is doing a lot of useful work on tackling inequality, states as one of its principles: 'Everyone in the UK should be able to live in affordable and high-quality housing (whether it is privately owned, privately rented, or in the social sector), with a market that operates transparently and where prices, quality and security of tenure are appropriately regulated.'[3]

Renting and poverty

The legal structure of tenancies is one thing, but, for thousands of renters, the problems they face are much more tangible: the unaffordability of their rent and the poor state of their housing.

For most people, private renting is not a cheap option. For those on the lowest incomes, it can be almost unaffordable due to the structure of the housing benefit system.

The Office for National Statistics issues data on the annual increase in private rents, and every month now it reports that the median figures 'are the highest ever recorded'.[4] Although rent rises slowed down during the pandemic, they have increased swiftly since 2021, with average new monthly rents reaching more than £2000 in London and £1000 outside the capital.

'Affordability' is generally accepted to mean housing costs taking up around a third of a household's income after tax, so on the whole these are at the limits of affordability for a household with two working adults (two well-paid working adults in London!).

Estate agency, Savills, takes the view that, with rents having risen by 26% since the start of the pandemic in 2020, they will reach an 'affordability ceiling' in 2025. The ceiling has already been hit in London, Savills suggests, where average rents typically take up more than 42% of the renter's income. Elsewhere, the average renting household is spending 35.3% of its income on rent.[5]

The independent Affordable Housing Commission, a non-partisan group made up of experts from across the housing sector, began an investigation in 2018 into why housing had become so unaffordable. In its 2020 report *Making Housing Affordable Again*, its chairman, Lord Best, said: 'After 18 months of studying the misery caused by housing affordability problems, the Affordable Housing Commission has not discovered a silver bullet that could fix everything. But we did unearth an underlying cause of so many households struggling with disproportionate housing costs: it is the switch into the private rented sector – which has more than doubled in size in less than twenty years – from both social renting and from home ownership.'[6]

The Commission set out its own definition of affordability: that housing costs should not exceed 33% of a household's net income, with that income figure allowing for family size and formation. 'We are particularly concerned at the numbers – mostly in the private rented sector – who are paying more than 40% of their net income for their housing,' the Commission said.

Since the Commission delivered this report in 2020, rents have moved remorselessly upwards and the impact on people on lower incomes is severe. A 2023 report from the Institute for Fiscal Studies (IFS), working with housing researchers at the independent Joseph Rowntree Foundation, shows the extent to which low-income families who, in the past, might have had access to social housing, are now relying on private renting and how this is dragging them further into poverty.[7]

Social and private renters have poverty rates of 46% and 34% respectively, compared with 12% for owner-occupiers, the IFS states. They are also far more likely to be materially deprived or to live in food insecurity.

'A steadily growing fraction of low-income households is in the private rented sector, while the share in social housing has declined, as has (in more recent years) the share who own their own home,' the report says. 'Younger generations of low-income individuals are now especially likely to be renting privately. For low-income adults born in the 1960s or before, private renting rates ranged from 5% to 20% at almost every age. But for those born in the 1970s it has persistently been in the 25-30% region, and for those born in the 1980s around 40-50%, as social renting and owner-occupation have declined. These patterns suggest that private renting will become even more common among low-income families going forward.'

The IFS points out that this matters because those in the private rented sector have higher housing costs than both social renters and homeowners with a mortgage, as well as having less security of tenure.

The IFS report reveals how dire the situation is for people claiming housing benefit. Its press release headline puts it in stark terms: 'Housing benefit has been frozen while rents have skyrocketed. Only 1 in 20 private rental properties on Zoopla can be covered by housing benefit.'

Around 38% of private renters claim housing benefit, but this is capped by Local Housing Allowances (LHA) – a limit on how much housing benefit a person can claim, depending on the local authority area. Except in certain circumstances (where the tenant is badly in arrears or has vulnerabilities, in which case it can be paid to the landlord), the housing benefit is paid directly to the tenant, whose responsibility it is to pay the full rent, even if the benefit payment is delayed or falls short.

LHAs have been frozen in cash terms since April 2020, while rents have risen hugely since then. The IFS analysis found that only 5% of homes were available at a rent housing benefit claimants could afford and that the problem was nationwide, not just in affluent areas. In some areas there were no rental properties at all available at or below the LHA.

Renters have to make up the shortfall from their own pocket or become homeless. All this is happening while people's non-housing costs go up as food and energy prices rise. A survey by Shelter and the Nationwide Building Society in November 2023 found that more than 800,000 private renters were under threat of eviction, mainly because they were unable to keep up with their rent.[8]

Both renters and landlords are finding things getting worse. The rise in mortgage interest rates has been a blow to Buy to Let landlords and they want to cover their costs by raising rents. Some are selling up and cashing in on house price rises; others are looking at the government's proposed reforms and perhaps thinking that being a landlord isn't so easy after all. Already in 2022, landlords sold 35,000 more properties than they bought. Surveys by The Royal Institution of Chartered Surveyors show tenant demand rising while new landlord instructions fall.[9]

The IFS report also examines how the affordability problem pushes low-income households into the worst properties. 'Low-income families in private rented properties are much more likely than social renters or owner-occupiers to be living in homes that are hazardous, in disrepair, difficult to adequately heat or lacking modern facilities,' it says. 'Around a quarter of private rented homes lived in by low-income people would fail the Decent Homes Standard that social rented properties are legally required to meet.'

Forcing poor people to rely on private renting is not only making them poorer but is also condemning them to worse living conditions.

In 2021, nearly 1m private rented homes failed to meet the Decent Homes Standard and, with the rise in energy costs, the consequences of having a damp, uninsulated home are severe. The IFS found that private rented properties that were cheap enough for low-income households to afford had 19% higher heating and hot water costs than the average.

Undoubtedly, the problem with a great many private rented properties is that they are just bad: cold, damp, unmodernised, in the worst cases afflicted with mould or vermin (or both).

The government itself acknowledges the implications of this, with the knock-on effect on people's health. In its proposals for the Renters (Reform) Bill, the Department for Levelling Up, Housing and Communities says: 'These dilapidated homes are costing the NHS an estimated £340m per annum and are holding back local areas, making them less attractive places to live and work.'

Bringing in the Decent Homes Standard for private rented properties would be an important step, but will negligent landlords invest the money? Or will they just sell up, or find ways of evading the requirements? Crucially, who will be checking up on them?

The government says it will give local authorities

extra enforcement powers, but this is ignoring the fact that a decade of cuts to local authority budgets has left councils with minimal abilities to regulate anything.

Generally, local authority environmental health officers (EHO) have the job of inspecting private rented accommodation under the Housing Health and Safety Rating System. Councils have the power to take action where properties are found to have hazards such as fire risks, damp and mould, or faulty gas boilers, but also problems like overcrowding or lack of heating.

The catch is that tenants have to ask for an inspection from the council and, in the words of the blunt warning to tenants on the Citizens Advice website: 'Your landlord may try to evict you if you complain.'[10]

Clearly a proper system of regular inspection by credible third parties would offer much greater protection to tenants and would act to raise standards in private rented properties. I believe it's vital to have a licensing system for private landlords, so that properties would have to be inspected, say annually, to ensure they are fit to be let out, and councils would also then know who the landlords are and where the properties are.

The 'Property Portal' in the Renters (Reform) Bill is proposed as a national register of landlords, allowing tenants to check that their prospective landlord has been approved by the local authority.

This is fine as far as it goes, but EHOs need powers to pursue the rogue landlords who are flying under the radar, and to impose penalties for abuses. They are also going to need money. The austerity cuts to local authority funding mean that council budgets for environmental health have been reduced by about 50% since 2009, and staffing levels cut by a third.[11] Environmental health departments have numerous statutory duties (such as dealing with public food standards, fly tipping and noise nuisance, as well as health and safety) so already there are fewer EHOs carrying out fewer inspections. They are not going to be able to make an impact on standards in private renting without the funding to do so.

The picture is the same throughout local authorities. The number of trading standards officers – who would be the ones to check on the validity of tenancy contracts – fell by between 30% and 50%, depending on the local authority, over the ten years to 2019.[12]

Regulation and licensing mean nothing without the resources to carry them out, so I believe the inspection scheme should be funded by a levy on landlords themselves, who would pay to be part of the scheme so that they can have their properties inspected and approved by their local authority. This would separate the good landlords from the bad and give renters the information they need to find a decent home.

The bad landlords won't go away, of course, so

local authorities need the powers to deal with them. Nevertheless, as long as social housing remains unavailable to people on very low incomes, there will be rogue landlords ready to take advantage of desperate tenants.

If there is any doubt that the private rented sector can be an abusive and dangerous place, a report by the National Audit Office (NAO) in May 2023 exposed the shocking extent to which vulnerable people can be exploited by rogue landlords. The NAO looked into the provision of supported housing, that is, housing for people who are living with disabilities or have had, say, mental health or addiction issues – essentially, people who need support in order to live independently and whose rents are usually covered by housing benefit.[13]

Astonishingly, it seems this whole area is largely unregulated and unscrupulous landlords have seen an opportunity to cash in. The NAO found local authorities didn't know exactly how many supported housing units were in their area. There is no direct regulation of the quality of support offered.

The housing itself can be dangerously substandard: one local authority told MPs in the Levelling Up, Housing and Communities Committee that in the 345 supported housing units it inspected between April 2019 and January 2022, it found 323 serious health and safety hazards. The Committee concluded that some residents' experiences of this type of accommodation were 'beyond disgraceful'.[14]

Yet landlords are making a profit from this housing, at the taxpayer's expense. The LHA caps on housing benefit don't apply to certain types of supported housing, so some landlords have been charging excessive rents.

That housing for the most vulnerable people in society can be exploited in this way is appalling. Yet this kind of situation will arise because the loopholes are there and also – fundamentally – because the lack of social housing means that people who ought to be in accommodation appropriate to their needs, with the support they are supposed to have, are being left instead to sink or swim in the unregulated private sector.

The only long-term answer is a greater supply of secure and genuinely affordable social housing.

CHAPTER 7

Land and planning: the price of permission

In this country, there is much talk about housing, but little about land. The vast majority of people in Britain don't own any land, other than (for homeowners) the plot their house and garden sit on (and they might not even own that if they've been sold a long lease).

The shocking fact, revealed by Guy Shrubsole in his book *Who Owns England?* is that well under 1% of the population of England own half the land. A few thousand individuals – the aristocracy, landed gentry and new owners, such as city bankers – own at least 47% of land, probably more, while corporations own another 18%. Land ownership is shrouded in secrecy and it has taken detailed research by Shrubsole and others to find this information.[1]

As a result of this concentration of ownership in the hands of a tiny minority, the rest of us generally don't have much idea about land values and we have very little say in how the land around us is used.

Yet land use is hugely important in our crowded country, and the crises we face make it even more important. We have a limited amount of land to accommodate everything that is vital for us: housing; businesses; transport; the farms we need to feed people; and space for a healthy natural environment to combat the climate and ecological emergencies (and for our own wellbeing). But land is the most finite resource of all – they're not making any more of it!

In a small country, these land uses compete against each other and a workable balance has to be achieved. Britain is not a place where we can have a Wild West free-for-all on land use, which is why we have a planning system. Unfortunately, planning has become one of the most criticised of public services, blamed for all sorts of ills, and debate about planning – whether at local or national government level – quickly gets polarised.

Time and again, politicians blame 'planning' for the shortfall in housing provision, implying that if only councils dished out more planning permissions (especially for building on greenbelt land) the problem would be solved.

At its party conference in October 2023, Labour announced its five-point plan for dealing with the housing crisis – and it appears to have fallen into the same trap of assuming the problems can be solved via the planning system.

Labour says it will have 'a housing recovery plan; a blitz of planning reform to quickly boost housebuilding to buy and rent and deliver the biggest boost to affordable housing in a generation.'[2]

I am sceptical that 'a blitz of planning reform' can achieve much. David Cameron's Conservative government tried this with a plan to loosen planning regulations and not much happened, apart from a storm of protest about saving the countryside.

Planning is the favoured scapegoat for politicians and housebuilders alike. Labour's press release points the finger: 'The Conservative government has allowed planning permissions to collapse to a record low because they are too weak to stand up to their backbenchers, members, and cronies whose interests are best served by limiting the supply of housing to buy and rent. Planning permissions have dropped to their lowest on record and, by the time of the next general election, new home completions are forecast to have dropped to as little as 160,000 per year.'

Planning permissions have certainly dwindled. The Home Builders Federation, representing private sector housebuilders and developers, reported that the number of projects granted planning permission during the second quarter of 2023 was 10% lower than the previous quarter and a 20% drop year on year.[3]

However, figures from the Department for Levelling Up, Housing and Communities suggest the fall is more to do with a drop in planning applications, than with councils refusing permissions. Local authorities received fewer applications to build new buildings or improve old ones in 2022 than at any point since 2006.[4]

The government made changes in the Levelling-Up and Regeneration Bill in 2023 that were intended to boost the volume of housebuilding, but at the same time removed the requirement for local authorities to set housebuilding targets.[5] Developers say the uncertainty caused is deterring new building, not helping it.

Clearly, whatever the reasons, fewer planning applications mean fewer homes being built. But, as far as I can see, building those homes would make little difference to our current housing disaster anyway.

Years of tinkering with the planning system has not achieved much. I'm not saying planning isn't important. A robust planning system is vital if new homes are to be built in the right places and with the consent of local communities.

But putting the onus on the planning system to solve the housing crisis is based on the assumption that there is a simple equation: if only more planning permissions were granted, more houses would be built and homes would become more affordable.

This assumption ignores two very obvious and interlinked points: firstly, with average house prices now running at more than eight times average full-time earnings[6] – in other words, way beyond what most people can get a mortgage for – increasing the number of homes built is not going to make any difference to the hundreds of thousands who want to buy a place of their own. It might give them more choice of properties to rent but it won't make a house any more affordable for them to buy. If increasing supply ever does bring prices down, it will take years for things to return to the state they were before 2000, when prices were typically three or four times earnings, making mortgages feasible and within the reach of working people.

Secondly, as is obvious, housebuilders have no real wish to build more and thereby reduce sale prices.

As I quoted in chapter 3, according to the Local Government Association, planning permission already exists for a million new homes that have not been built because developers have chosen not to build them yet. Restricting the numbers of homes they build, to keep prices high, brings enormous gains for developers. I very much doubt if well-intentioned local housing plans, setting higher targets for the supply of new homes and the proportion of 'affordable' homes (even if these were genuinely affordable), will make much difference to developers' business models.

The real planning issues: land value capture and the price of permission

Although I don't believe the planning system holds all the answers, the housing crisis cannot be tackled without a rational and intelligent look at land and planning. It seems to me there are some serious issues that are not being talked about, the most important of which is that we need to find a workable way of achieving land value capture.

The Organisation for Economic Co-operation and Development defines land value capture as 'a policy approach that enables communities to recover and reinvest land value increases that result from public investment and government actions.'[7] Government actions here would include the granting of planning permission. At the moment, the measures we have to get something back for the community when developments go ahead are feeble. It is no wonder that proposals for new housing developments often meet local opposition when communities have to bear many of the downsides of a new development and see little benefit for themselves (not to mention that the people in the area who most need housing can't afford to buy the new properties being built).

I find it scandalous that planning permission – which controls how land, our precious and finite resource, is used – is effectively given away to developers who take the profits and give virtually nothing to the community in return for it.

We need to address the whole issue of land compensation and how it puts the interests of landowners and developers above those of people needing housing. Currently, the system stands in the way of achieving genuinely affordable housing. Landowners and developers win, communities lose.

After the Second World War, the government brought in several measures to get a housebuilding programme up and running quickly. The Town and Country Planning Act 1947 introduced local authority planning, which is the basis of the system we still have. For the first time, landowners had to get permission from the local council to develop their land.

The Labour government of the day recognised that planning permission has a significant monetary value; a field has far more value when houses can be built on it, for profit, than it does when its only residents are cows. Therefore, the government took the view that there ought to be a tax on the unearned windfall landowners would receive after being granted planning permission so it imposed a 'development charge' of 100% of the increase in the land value after planning permission had been granted. In other words, the owner couldn't make a profit from selling the land for housing.

But this development charge was short-lived. It proved to be counter-productive, as Guy Shrubsole explains in *Who Owns England?*, as landowners had no incentive to sell, and private housebuilding slowed down. When there was a change of government and the Conservatives came in, they scrapped the development charge in 1953 and it has never been replaced with anything.

As a result, we have the situation where the windfall increase in land value, which is granted by planning permission, is not taxed. Effectively the state, via the local authority planning department, gives the landowner that very valuable uplift for free.

At the same time, every housing development has implications for its local area – some beneficial (more customers for local businesses) but many putting pressure on local services. More households mean more cars (more traffic and pollution, more parked vehicles taking up space). They mean more children at local schools (though in some areas that is welcome), more people wanting a GP appointment and so on. Without major funding, councils are not in a position to scale up services to meet demand. This has always been an issue, but the problem has become acute, now that local authority services have been cut to the bone by austerity measures.

If we are going to increase substantially the provision of housing, with all the roads, services, utilities and so on to go with it, requiring major infrastructure investment, then some sort of land value capture is essential.

As a citizen, I feel very strongly that the way planning permission (which I regard as an asset of the state) is practically given away, is wrong. Planning permission must no longer be a free gift. It is a valuable state asset, which must be priced or taxed accordingly, and developers should pay.

Other countries – such as the Netherlands – have a system for doing this, but it seems to me that in the UK the voices of landowners and developers have taken precedence, so nothing has been done to make them contribute a fair share of the financial consequences of their developments, or of the enormous profits this planning permission will generate for them.

Many experts have examined the issue of land value capture and there is no lack of informed thinking on the subject. Inevitably, various ideas all have their pluses and minuses, but doing nothing seems unacceptable in the housing (and public finance) crisis we're in.

The biggest obstacle is, undoubtedly, politics. The Scottish Government has been more open to looking at land issues and has set up the Scottish Land Commission. One of the things it looked at is land value capture and what might be learned from past attempts, and from the ways other countries do things. 'Most of the uplift in land values arising from planning permission remains uncaptured by the state,' the Commission's 2018 report says.[8] But it warns: 'Past attempts at land value capture have failed largely due to the absence of political consensus to support them. The lesson is that political consensus, based on an understanding of the principles underpinning land value capture, should be established before any major initiative is taken. Connected to this, schemes should be seen to be fair in order to command public consent.'

So we need the will to do this and that is what I'm desperate to encourage here.

Section 106 falls short

The main form of land value capture that we currently have is via section 106 (s106) of the Town and Country Planning Act 1990, whereby councils granting planning permission for a development can ask for a percentage of the project to be put into affordable housing or used to pay for some other community facility. How effective this is probably depends on the council's negotiating skills. Many local authorities have parlayed s106 into actual affordable housing built within a new development; others seem to have ended up with little more than a children's playground on a leftover bit of land.

S106 agreements are one of the few tools local authorities have at their disposal to get affordable housing built in their area, and governments have been keen to encourage this. The agreement can require that a proportion of units built in a new development be 'affordable'. A recent report by the New Economics Foundation (NEF) found that: 'Through s106, in 2018-19, local authorities got £7bn in developer contributions, with 90% of local planning authorities attaching conditions to planning permission for new developments.' As a result: '47.7% of affordable housing in England built in 2020-21, over 24,800 units' came about through s106 agreements.[9]

This sounds good, but it depends what is meant by 'affordable'. It can mean schemes such as shared ownership, but usually it means some sort of discounted price, which, in today's market, brings the property nowhere near within the reach of people on moderate incomes. The National Planning Policy Framework defines 'affordable' as a property rented at a minimum of 20% below local market rents, or a property for sale at 20% below market prices.[10] Thus you get the ridiculous situation that an apartment in the new developments at Canary Wharf can be deemed 'affordable' if it costs £800,000 rather than £1m.

Too often, the reality is simply that developers say to the planning authority that their scheme isn't viable at the levels of s106 requested. They negotiate it down and the amount of affordable housing included is reduced. This is what happened at the overblown Battersea Power Station development, where the initial promise of 15% affordable housing (a very small figure for an area desperately in need of housing) was further negotiated down to 9% by the developers pleading it was not financially viable to include any more.[11]

Whichever way you look at it, s106 used in this way delivers little for the community. In my opinion, it is a discredited system, leaving too much reliant on the negotiating abilities of short-staffed local authority planning departments, who are up against the well-resourced legal teams of the developer firms. S106 agreements are a poor way of getting affordable housing (even supposing this is actually affordable) and will rarely do anything to address a local area's real housing needs.

It is interesting that the problems with s106 have been acknowledged by the Labour party in its proposals to boost affordable housing. The party says it would prevent developers 'wriggling out' of s106 obligations by introducing an expert unit to give councils and housing associations advice on negotiating with property firms.

This might help, but it seems to me s106 agreements will only ever deliver marginal benefits and are not a serious way to provide genuinely affordable housing.

One strength of the s106 system is that it operates locally, so such benefits as exist are visible to the community – but this also creates inequity. As the NEF notes: 'With s106, affordable housing is delivered via the success of private housing developments... This means the state of the market, not local need, determines where affordable housing is delivered. Of the £7bn secured in s106 developer contributions in 2018-19, the majority were in the more affluent south of England.'

In addition to s106, there is the Community Infrastructure Levy (CIL), introduced by the Labour government, which came into force in 2010.[12] This allows local authorities in England and Wales to raise funds from developers undertaking new building projects in their area. The idea is that the money can fund a wide range of the infrastructure needed as a result of development. Promoting the CIL, the government gave an ambitious list of infrastructure that could benefit: 'new or safer road schemes, flood defences, schools, hospitals and other health and social care facilities, park improvements, green spaces and leisure centres.'

The CIL was introduced in response to a recognition that s106 wasn't working. 'The Community Infrastructure Levy is fairer, faster and more certain and transparent than the system of planning obligations which causes delay as a result of lengthy negotiations... only 6% of all planning permissions brought any contribution to the cost of supporting infrastructure, when even small developments can create a need for new services,' the government said at the time.

The CIL was explicitly meant to encourage new development, presumably by giving councils an enhanced incentive to grant planning permission. Local authorities could choose whether to levy a CIL or not and it was not envisaged a CIL would be used to provide affordable housing as s106 could still be used for this.

In 2013, the Conservative government added a further measure as an extra incentive for housebuilding: in areas where there was a neighbourhood development plan in place, the neighbourhood would be able to receive 25% of the revenues from the CIL arising from the development that they had chosen to accept. The money would be paid directly to parish and town councils and could be used for community projects such as re-roofing a village hall, refurbishing a municipal pool, or taking over a community pub.

The idea was that this would be a way to overcome local objections to new housing developments and thereby increase housing provision.

Despite all these intentions, the CIL doesn't seem to have been enormously effective. A study commissioned by the government in 2015 found that less than a third of councils were using CILs by that point and that they were lengthy and expensive to administer. Any revenue from them was reduced by numerous exemptions and reliefs. As with s106, CILs worked best in affluent areas with high market values for land.[13]

Where large, mixed-tenure schemes built by commercial developers have included some housing sold to housing associations at a discount, the housing associations have often been frustrated that CIL money, supposedly for infrastructure, is not used to support public transport. A new housing development on an edge-of-town, former greenfield site tends to rely on the residents having cars: social housing tenants on low incomes are more likely to depend on public transport and they're reluctant to accept housing where they can't get to work.

The original goal had been for CILs to be raising an estimated additional £1bn a year of funding for local infrastructure by 2016. The actual results don't seem to have come anywhere near this and the only place where a CIL has really worked is London, where high land prices and a development boom mean that the levy on planning permission has brought in large sums. Consequently, the Mayoral CIL levied from 2012 made a large contribution to funding Transport for London's new Elizabeth line.[14]

Once again, linking funding to the land and housing market means that poorer areas of the country – which might desperately need better infrastructure – are the least likely to benefit.

One thing is clear: planning obligations are not the way to secure genuinely affordable housing. In fact, trying to make communities agree to more planning permissions for private developments, via small incentives like a promised new roof for the village hall, is irrelevant and ineffectual in the face of the housing crisis facing us. Developers continue to make huge profits and the local housing waiting list remains unchanged.

Indeed, I would advise a moratorium on all planning permission given to large-scale developments in any areas where there is a social housing waiting list of consequence. If planning permission is subsequently allowed for those projects, then the developer should pay a price that more fairly reflects the value of the asset they have been granted and the funds should be channelled directly into social housing.

I would propose that, going forwards, all

planning permission should be sold at fixed and transparent prices. As with shopping in a supermarket, the customer (in this case the developer) pays the prices asked.

Prices would be linked to both the size of the property and the neighbourhood, so planning permission for a 50 square metre apartment in Chelsea would cost a lot more than a 100 square metre house in Hull. The values for each borough would be agreed annually, linked to inflation and any other factors, and that would be the price paid. The asset uplift would now be received by the local authority, to the benefit of the council taxpayer, while the builder takes the profit from the construction process.

This would replace the much-discredited s106 and would be a clear and consistent cost on development. It would cover contributions to the council for local facilities and, ideally, the sums raised would also go towards funding social housing.

A Community Infrastructure Levy should still be charged to the developer as well, on a cost-plus basis, for the direct costs to the community of necessary road changes, sewerage system improvements and so on, which arise because of the new development.

A better way to get affordable housing

There is a way to address affordability at source and, again, it comes back to land. Serious problems today originate from Harold Macmillan's Land Compensation Act of 1961, which I believe we urgently need to repeal.

The post-war Labour government gave local authorities the power to acquire land at 'existing use value' and by compulsory purchase if necessary. This meant that when they acquired land for housebuilding, they paid the current value of the land (generally its value as agricultural land). The owner would not be compensated for the land's 'hope value' – the price the landowner would hope to get by selling it for housing.

Acquiring land at this lower price meant that councils could build housing more cheaply and therefore let the homes at genuinely affordable rents. This system operated for 11 years and, during that time, Guy Shrubsole reports, 'about 1.8 m council houses were constructed in England – a third of all the council housing built in this country since the Second World War.'

New town development corporations, set up by the New Towns Act of 1946, were empowered to acquire land in the same way, with the result that 21 new towns, such as Stevenage, Harlow and Corby, were built in the 1950s on land purchased at prices reflecting its then use, which was mainly agricultural.

For a while, both Labour and the Conservatives agreed this was the best way to get housing constructed economically and quickly. But, Shrubsole writes, 'the landowners and developers won out in the end.'

Their lobbying for higher compensation led to the Land Compensation Act 1961, which meant that landowners would henceforward be compensated for the *potential* value of their land.

This, in one fell swoop, meant that no new towns, or indeed any housing schemes of scale, could be viably built due to the new exorbitant cost of the land. A site with planning permission for housing is worth up to three hundred times more than agricultural land. As a consequence, the new town movement as such had largely fizzled out by 1970. Every now and then there is talk of 'new towns' being built (such as Northstowe near Cambridge, currently half built) but these appear to be essentially large private housing estates.

My argument is that we need an extensive programme of social housing construction: nothing else will solve the country's severe housing crisis. Where local authorities (or whatever bodies are tasked with doing this) have to acquire land for development, it should be done in such a way that the housing scheme is financially viable and the taxpayer is not forced to put vast sums of extra money in the pockets of landowners.

This means repealing the Land Compensation Act and allowing councils to acquire land at existing use value. Where the land has to be compulsorily purchased, it may be appropriate to remove the Capital Gains Tax liability or uplift the current use value by, say, 50-100% as a generous sweetener to vendors.

Paying existing use value would take a huge cost out of the equation. Land for housing could be bought for, say, £10,000 an acre (the average value of prime arable land) instead of the up to £3m an acre it can cost now. Councils would be able to buy significant amounts of land, which would ultimately turn on the massive supply tap of housing that we need at relatively minimal cost. It would be possible to build social housing to be let at rents significantly below market rents. Think of the savings this would mean for households and for the state, which pays out billions in housing benefit every year.

At the same time there would be an enormous asset uplift to the UK's balance sheet as formerly agricultural land becomes residential. In other words, the whole country will benefit from the asset uplift instead of private developers making the gain through acquiring planning permission for free.

Land matters

There is no doubt that land use is a deeply political issue and I am entering controversial territory with my proposals on planning and land compensation, although I have no political axe to grind.

In 2019 Labour issued a discussion paper, *Land for the Many*, which looked in depth at the inequities of land issues.[15] The report's preface says: 'Dig deep enough into many of the problems this country faces, and you will soon hit land. Soaring inequality and exclusion; the massive cost of renting or buying a decent home; repeated financial crises, sparked by housing asset bubbles; the collapse of wildlife and ecosystems; the lack of public amenities – the way land is owned and controlled underlies them all. Yet it scarcely features in political discussions. The sense that even in discussing land we are trespassing is so strong that this critical issue remains off the agenda. Yet we cannot solve our many dysfunctions without addressing it.'

I would argue that we do have to trespass on this forbidden territory. If we do not address it and come up with workable solutions to the issues of land value and land use, we cannot tackle the housing crisis that ordinary people are suffering. Most members of the public may never be landowners but that doesn't mean they don't deserve a decent and genuinely affordable place to live.

CHAPTER 8

Making better use of buildings and land

Can we tackle the housing crisis by using what we have more efficiently? In other words – must the extra homes we need be newly built on greenfield sites, or can we meet demand by bringing empty homes back into use and constructing on brownfield sites?

It's highly likely that 'using what we already have' would be more popular with the general public and local politicians than the approach of relaxing planning laws and getting more houses built on greenfield sites. New developments on greenfield sites tend to cause political tensions locally, whereas communities like to see scruffy brownfield sites and redundant properties restored to use. This kind of development improves the look of an area, helps regenerate the economy and brings life into town centres.

But are there enough unused homes and brownfield sites to make a difference to the housing crisis? Are they in the places where people actually need homes? And can they be done cost-effectively?

Empty homes

It's widely recognised that empty homes are a problem to be addressed. I don't mean the percentage of empty properties that will always be in the system: second homes, homes being done up, or those waiting to be sold or rented. The waste is in homes that are standing empty long-term, unavailable or unfit to live in.

Wales and Scotland have both been proactive here, with the Welsh Government currently offering grants to help property owners bring places back into use.[1] The Scottish Government is working with Shelter to create the Scottish Empty Homes Partnership, focused on bringing empty homes back into use, where possible, as affordable housing.[2] England does not have a national programme, but the government does publish data every year on numbers of vacant dwellings. For 2022 the total for England was put at 676,304 – a figure which is 100,000 less than in 2009 but which has been mounting steadily since 2016.[3]

Of these, a relatively small number, just under 33,000, were council properties, about half of which were available for letting. So the problem is largely in privately owned properties.

A recent report by Leeds Building Society analysing the figures noted that around 250,000 of the vacant properties had been empty for more than six months.[4] It also found a north-south divide when looking at the vacancy figures by region: although the north-east had the lowest number of empty properties, its figure was the highest as a percentage of total homes in the region, at 3.3%. London had the lowest percentage, at 2.4%.

This is what you'd expect as it reflects the economic health of each region and therefore the demand for housing. On the whole, where housing is expensive, it is worth owners' whiles to make their properties available for rent or sale. There are other parts of the country where industry has departed, the population is declining and homes stand empty.

That's why looking at overall figures can be misleading. It's no good saying we can house people needing homes in those 670,000 empty properties if the properties are not the kind of homes, or in the kind of places, where people want them.

That said, there are people who need housing in every part of the country and bringing empty homes back into use ought to be part of the solution.

The Leeds Building Society report notes that there are other long-term benefits from tackling empty properties, as well as the priority of housing people now. Bringing vacant dwellings back into use should also mean taking the opportunity to bring them up to modern, energy-efficient standards.

'Re-purposing and retrofitting our existing housing stock – including empty homes – should be a key government priority,' the report says. 'Empty homes come in all shapes and sizes. They include derelict homes as well as homes that just need some slight renovation. Some of these empty homes are in a very bad state of repair, but many of them are in a reasonable condition. Recent estimates show that the average empty home only needs around £20,000 spending on it to make it habitable once again.'

This makes sense in other ways too. According to Mike Berners-Lee's book *How Bad Are Bananas? The Carbon Footprint of Everything*, building a new home has a carbon footprint of 80 tonnes of CO_2. But refurbishing an old house carries much less of a carbon footprint, equating to just 8 tonnes of CO_2.[5]

The campaign, Action on Empty Homes, which runs an Empty Homes Week every year, claims there are more like 1m homes standing empty.[6] It argues that the official total of 676,000 empty homes is not the full picture, saying in its 2023 campaign: 'This figure excludes a further 257,000 so-called 'second homes' or 'furnished empties' and over 70,000 second homes flipped to paying business rates as permanent short-lets.'

I think we need to be careful as it is easy to whip up rage against second homes. Some of these properties will be a genuine part of the tourism industry and regularly used; others may stand empty apart from the occasional weekend. There has been a boom in second-home buying in the UK. Second homes are subject to a higher rate of stamp duty and council tax and there has been a 20% rise in the sale of homes paying this higher stamp duty.[7] Possibly Brexit and Covid have pushed people with disposable wealth to opt for holiday homes in this country, but arguments continue as to whether this is a good thing or a bad thing for our rural and seaside economies. In areas such as, for example, parts of Cornwall and Devon, owners of holiday homes are accused of driving up house prices and taking properties out of circulation while council housing waiting lists grow.

Undoubtedly there is a real problem of homes being unaffordable for local people to buy or rent and it is not surprising that feelings run high. But we live in a democracy, and I can't see how we can stop people legitimately buying and maintaining a property, bought at the prevailing market price with 'clean', tax-paid money, to use as they wish. Besides, in areas with a tourism economy, a good supply of holiday cottages to let is essential if visitors are to be accommodated and spend their money in the area. I would argue that in these parts of the country, particularly as wages tend to be low in rural areas, the real problem goes back to the lack of long-term housing at genuinely affordable rents.

Why are homes left empty?

There could be many reasons for homes being vacant.

Are the places empty because the owner can't afford to do them up, or maybe because local rents are not high enough for the owner to think it worthwhile? Are some of these properties owned by large companies that take no interest in them, but just have them on the books as assets? Are the owners leaving them empty, waiting for them to go up in value so they can sell?

Only a local approach is going to work here, to get to the bottom of these questions. Councils need more powers (and money) to investigate and deal with empty properties. They have Empty Dwelling Management Orders as a legal instrument but, currently, the use of these orders is restricted to cases where the property has become dangerous or is being used for anti-social activity (such as drug dealing).

Getting vacant homes back into use is not going to give us the numbers we need to solve the housing crisis, but it could make a useful contribution. A way needs to be found to do it without penalising owners who have genuine plans for a property that is currently vacant, or who just don't have the funds to make it habitable. Given the nature of England's housing stock, a lot of these properties are going to be a century old. Perhaps some sort of empty property fund is needed, from which owners could borrow to restore the dwelling and bring it up to modern safety and energy-efficiency standards. It would be a worthwhile investment in improving the nation's housing stock.

Many empty homes, though, are not dilapidated Edwardian terraces but modern apartments, which links to another element in our dysfunctional housing system.

Policymakers are pinning their hopes on the fabled '300,000 homes' to be built, yet many new developments make no dent at all in the levels of housing need. This is because the properties are not actually lived in but fall into that investment property category.

In major cities and the south of England, where there is high housing demand, there is no lack of construction going on. But luxury canalside flats and executive homes on greenfield sites are of no use to the homeless. They are of use to investors, but, perversely, the over-pressured housing market means that there is no need to rent out those properties in order to make money: you simply leave them vacant or put them on very short lets and wait for the value to go up. Rather than 'Buy to Let', the owners prefer to 'Buy to Leave' (especially when the yield is relatively poor and the biggest gain comes from increases in capital value, without the wear and tear to the property of a tenant living in it).

Mayor of London Sadiq Khan and Westminster City Council have recently been calling for stronger powers to crack down on empty homes, estimating there are 30,000 long-term empty homes across London.[8] They would like to have the power to levy higher rates of council tax on these properties and to be able to use Empty Dwelling Management Orders to temporarily take over long-term vacant homes. Current rates of council tax are no deterrent for wealthy owners to leave places standing vacant. Higher rates might not be a deterrent either, but would at least raise funds to tackle homelessness.

The highest concentration of empty properties is in the Royal Borough of Kensington and Chelsea, where 1,600 empty properties would collectively be worth more than £2.2bn, such is the value of property in central London. The value is high, but the actual numbers of empty properties are not great relative to the size of London. However, it is a serious issue and one that is getting worse as there are now 10,000 more long-term empty properties in the capital than there were in 2019.[9] At the same time, private rents have surged to new heights and London boroughs are under such intense pressure that they are housing homeless families outside the city (a controversial policy), so the existence of empty homes is strongly resented.

I dislike the weird situation in London, where the most exclusive and sought-after streets can also be the most empty and lifeless. These expensive neighbourhoods are a victim of their own success, with properties – both classic townhouses and new high-rise developments – bought by international investors who have no intention of living there nor have any incentive to let anyone else live there.[10] Campaigners have highlighted the bizarre case of a site on The Bishop's Avenue, north London, one of the most expensive streets in Britain, where mansions owned by an Isle of Man-registered company with a Dubai address are not only empty but have been derelict for years. The site is so big that architects say 300 affordable homes could be built on it.[11]

In reality, London (and no doubt other cities) is full of empty dwellings which could be of more use to the average family than a billionaire's mansion would be. In August 2023, protestors occupied 28 flats in Camden that used to be for prison officers at HMP Pentonville, but which have been left empty for 10 years.[12] The short sit-in aimed to draw attention to the fact that these were family-sized homes, being wasted by their owner, the government. Maybe not everyone would be keen to live next to a prison, but in the current rental market, many people would not be fussy.

Another key question is: how many of these empty houses (and other properties in London and elsewhere) are being owned by tax avoiders and criminals? It is well known that owning property can be a means of dodging tax and laundering money, and England is wide open to this because of our failure to crack down on the owning of property through offshore trusts.

There have been a lot of media revelations about Russian oligarchs who have been found to own property in London. But they are not the only ones taking advantage of the UK's lax laws. Investing in property through an offshore trust is a favoured method for those who secrete money out of the UK to evade tax and then bring it back again in the form of 'offset' loans (where money is borrowed from offshore banks using the questionable cash as security). These mechanisms have been exposed by campaigners like Richard Brooks, whose book *The Great Tax Robbery* revealed the elaborate dodges created by the ultra-wealthy and their accountants and advisers.[13] In 2018, with Richard Brooks, I set up the investigative think-tank TaxWatch UK[14] to report on issues of tax compliance, and the researchers there have done much digging into tax fraud and avoidance.

Others using offshore trusts are crime syndicates laundering their cash, corrupt politicians spending their ill-gotten gains, or overseas felons escaping justice to a safe haven where professionals have failed to ask any questions as to the source of their funds. This does have consequences for ordinary people as offshore buyers have pushed up prices in London with knock-on effects all along the property chain.

As part of the Economic Crime (Transparency and Enforcement) Act, in November 2022 the government brought in a 'register of overseas entities', which is supposed to force overseas companies to reveal the true owner of any properties in England and Wales bought in the past 20 years. The penalty for non-compliance is fines or prison. This move has been talked about for years, but the legislation was finally rushed through Parliament after Russia's invasion of Ukraine. It has been estimated that there are 95,000 UK properties held by 32,000 overseas companies.

However, legal experts and campaigners say the new law is weak. Labour MP Margaret Hodge, who has long campaigned for a crackdown on secretive overseas ownership of UK property, has said: 'The new register is riddled with flaws and loopholes. To truly stop the flows of corrupt wealth into our housing market, the government must urgently put in place an open register of the true owners of UK land and property, not just of those owned by companies.'

I would argue the easiest way is to simply stop companies and trusts from purchasing land, property, and businesses in this country unless they disclose their beneficial ownership and can demonstrate that the funds being used are legitimate and all taxes have been paid. Unexplained wealth orders, which commenced in January 2018, might also be used to require existing owners to explain their finances where there are doubts about the propriety.

Foreign ownership of UK homes is far more widespread than people realise and is not confined to mansions in Hampstead. In 2018 *The Guardian* reported on the scandal of an ex-council tower block in Liverpool which, after being sold off by the local authority, became 80% owned by overseas speculators from countries including Russia, Saudi Arabia, and Australia.[15] Flats continued to be let out to local people, most on housing benefit, but lack of investment in the homes led to environmental health inspectors declaring them unfit for habitation. The overseas owners had no interest in installing proper heating, for example, or making any improvements: they simply took the annual 8% return on their investment via the rents paid through benefits (which meant, effectively, via the taxpayer). It is shocking that in this country we are wide open to this sort of exploitation.

What about other buildings standing empty: could they be repurposed as homes? This would seem to be a real proposition, and something the government is keen to promote. Consultation launched by Housing Secretary Michael Gove in February 2024[16] proposes relaxing planning laws to 'extend current permitted development rights, so that commercial buildings of any size will have the freedom to be converted into new homes – this means shops, offices, and other buildings all quickly repurposed.'

This doesn't seem very groundbreaking as, in reality, commercial buildings (such as former warehouses and factories in urban areas) are frequently redeveloped for housing. Developers gave a lukewarm response: the proposal 'may help bring some vacant properties back into use but this is not a silver bullet for housing delivery,' Melanie Leech, chief executive of the British Property Federation, said. 'Only a small number of buildings are likely to be suitable for homes and it is paramount that there is effective 'quality control' in place to make sure that we do not end up with poor quality homes in our town centres.'[17]

The quality control issue is essential because, in fact, converting offices into homes is already happening and unfortunately the record so far is not good. In 2019, the BBC's Panorama reported on the shocking situation in Harlow, Essex, where a large, privately owned, high-rise office block, Terminus House, had been 'converted' into housing and filled with homeless families shipped there from several boroughs in and around London.[18] The local authority, Harlow District Council, had no say in this as the conversion was made without planning permission under the 'permitted development' law. This law, when introduced, was presented by the government as being a beneficial measure, generally about allowing people to build a larger conservatory, so clearly there needs to be some amendment closing the loopholes that allow abuses.

Residents of Terminus House told the BBC their living space was tiny and children had no outdoor space to play, plus they were frightened by the high level of crime and drug use in the block. Panorama found other former business premises in the town being used to house families. Not only was the situation bad inside the buildings but, because they were intended for business use, they were far from amenities such as shops and public transport.

I'm sure that, in principle, it is possible to convert office blocks into homes with the right kind of design and investment. They might not be as pretty and trendy as a warehouse conversion, but they could be perfectly functional. However, in this case what we have instead is an owner looking to make a fast buck by relying on guaranteed income from councils wanting to solve their homelessness problem. It is a cynical exercise when everyone knows the households placed there are powerless to complain.

Unused land

Bringing long-term vacant homes back into use will help ease the housing crisis, but if we are to get social housing in the quantities which I believe we need, in order to make a real difference, we have to build.

Wherever possible, we should be looking at brownfield rather than greenfield sites. However, some of the land for which planning permission has already been granted but on which no homes have yet been built (as I've mentioned in previous chapters) will be greenfield sites and, if they are a good site for social housing, they should be used.

Green belt – the land circling London and other cities, which was put in place to prevent conurbations spreading into one another – is a sensitive issue and one on which it is difficult to get an objective view. There are calls for the 'stranglehold' of green belt to be lifted, with proponents saying the rules were put in place in the 1950s and don't meet today's needs. However, often the people making this case turn out to be developers with their eye on the land.

On the other hand, some environmentalists have rejected the idea that it has to be 'housing versus nature'. Tony Juniper, the chair of Natural England, says the 'oppositional mindset' is not helping communities, who need both housing and green space. Instead, he says, we should be 'thinking more about how we can accommodate high-quality nature within and around residential developments, not only in order to meet nature targets, but also in order to promote social wellbeing.[19]

It seems to me that the green belt is often just a political football rather than regarded rationally. Politicians defend the green belt when they think doing so will be a vote winner, yet the government has allowed HS2 to destroy thousands of acres of green belt land. Meanwhile, the libertarian think tank, the Adam Smith Institute, has argued that extending development into the green belt in just a half-mile strip around London would provide land for 800,000 new homes.[20]

We must decide as a society whether, in some places, the loss of green belt is a price worth paying – but we should also ask whether the developments that result do anything to help meet our real housing needs.

Local communities are often attached to their green belt, even though in many cases this land is not some rural idyll but messy scraps of green among major roads, power lines, industry and so on. One person's 'wasted' site is another person's favourite dog-walking field. But people might well agree that the sites could be usefully used for housing if they felt that they would gain as a community from the development in terms of meaningfully affordable housing, or in terms of getting some significant contribution to local infrastructure, such as a new school rather than it just being a way for large companies to make a profit.

The government's own adviser on building and planning, Nicholas Boys Smith, has said not all of the green belt should be 'preserved in aspic forever', when younger generations are being failed by the lack of new homes. 'As a society we have fallen out of love with the future and we have… under both political parties failed to build enough homes. Clearly, we need to look at the quality of land within green belts and think which of this should be preserved,' he said.[21]

Boys Smith acknowledged that building on green belt land is unpopular, but he argued that this was often down to poor design, with too many developments being ill thought out and unloved by the public.

Green belts are being eaten into all the time by planning creep as towns and cities expand. What I object to is the way developers profit from this by taking options with farmers on land surrounding towns and counting on the local housing plan extending into this area, so they can capitalise on the huge rise in land values, which is a state asset they don't deserve, as I've discussed in chapter 7.

However, proposals to use green belt land will always be highly political and can lead to long-running rows, proposals and appeals, probably lasting years. This is no help when we need housing now.

So where can we look for land that is readily usable?

Brownfield sites should be used wherever possible, and they are to be found everywhere.

Again, this is something the government is now pursuing in its new consultation paper: the Department for Levelling Up, Housing and Communities says, 'every council in England will be told that they will need to prioritise brownfield developments and instructed to be less bureaucratic and more flexible in applying policies that halt housebuilding on brownfield land... Planning authorities in England's 20 largest cities and towns will be made to follow a "brownfield presumption".'

These proposals seem to take for granted, as I've noted before, that planning refusals are to blame for the housing crisis. The more likely reason, though, that more housebuilding isn't taking place on brownfield sites is that it can be expensive. The sites are often awkward, hard to access, polluted and need clearing first. That is why developers prefer nice, open greenfield sites, which are so much easier and cheaper to build on. If brownfield sites are to be brought into use, funds will be needed as many former industrial sites require major investment to be cleaned up and brought into use.

Putting public sector property to use

Over the past 10 years, government departments have been encouraged to sell off surplus land and, in some cases, this has been used for major housing developments, for example on former army or airforce bases.

However, an investigation in 2020 by the New Economics Foundation (NEF) suggested that the sell-off was adding to the housing crisis rather than alleviating it.[22] The NEF's report noted that the government's five-year programme had the dual aim of releasing enough land for 160,000 homes by 2020 and raising £5bn in capital receipts. But, while the land has been sold, the government has not ensured that the properties built will do anything to solve the housing crisis.

'Our analysis has found that while the government has sold enough public land for developers to build 131,000 homes, only 2.6% of those homes will be for social rent,' the NEF said. Of the homes built on sold-off public land, 15% are classified as 'affordable housing'. However, the government does not have data on what kind of affordable housing this is, the

NEF pointed out. Since the definition of 'affordable' includes homes sold or rented at 80% of market rates, most of these homes could be way out of reach for people on low incomes.

This has led to the crazy situation where homes built on former NHS land are unaffordable to NHS staff – at a time when hospitals have a recruitment and retention crisis because their employees cannot afford to live near their workplace!

Many NHS trusts have been selling surplus land since a 2017 review of NHS property and estates by Sir Robert Naylor advocated disposing of NHS land to enable the delivery of 26,000 new homes.[23]

This sounds good, except that the NEF found that the average sale price of houses built on NHS land was 9.6 times the average annual salary of a nurse.[24] Only 5% of the homes built on sold-off NHS land are for genuinely affordable social rent.

Undoubtedly the health service needs the money. But its staff also need homes, and we, as a nation, need those staff. An organisation called the NHS Homes Alliance (made up of NHS trusts, housing associations, architects, and developers) now argues that 'selling the family silver' for commercial developments is the wrong approach and, instead, NHS trusts should retain the freehold on their brownfield sites and explore alternative means of redeveloping them to deliver homes for health and social care staff.[25]

The state needs a different mentality. For a

decade, the government has encouraged (or ordered) bodies to sell off their land at the highest possible price in order to ease public finances. But this has meant that virtually none of the land goes for social housing and, in the long term, the result will be more cost to the public purse – from recruitment and staffing shortages, from the health problems suffered by people in inadequate accommodation, from the bill to local authorities for housing homeless families in temporary accommodation, and so on.

The Church of England seems to have the same mentality. It is one of the major landowners in England: Guy Shrubsole's book estimates the church, its dioceses and the Church Commissioners altogether have about 350,000 acres. The archbishops' report, *Coming Home*, makes an impassioned plea for helping people in housing need and does feature some small local projects where churches are taking action, but I searched the report in vain for the church making any long-term commitment to action as a landowner. Just making 100 acres of surplus church land a year available for social housing would have an impact. It would not even need to sell the land but would make it available for the development of housing to be let at genuinely affordable rents.

While 100 acres might not sound a lot, it could have a significant impact. Given that 100 flats can be built on one acre, 100 acres provides space for 10,000 social homes to be built. To my mind, this would be fully in line with the church's mission. Yes, there is a lower total return if homes are let at social rents rather than sold or let at market rents, but the difference is only 2% or so and the benefits to society of genuinely affordable rents are huge.

We need to come round to a recognition that providing enough good-quality, secure housing, that people can afford, is not a drain on the finances but a vital investment in the country's future.

If land owned by public bodies, charities and quangos that is currently up for disposal were allocated for the building of social rented housing rather than being sold on the open market, that would immediately start to make a dent in the social housing shortage.

We've seen how the NHS, and no doubt many other public bodies and charities, are taking refuge behind the argument that their 'obligation' to the taxpayer is to get the highest price possible from their assets. Let's turn that on its head and say that their obligation is to facilitate something that will make an enormous difference to the health and wellbeing of people in this country – the provision of decent, secure, genuinely affordable housing.

CHAPTER 9

Building a solution

The housing crisis in this country runs deep – deeper than most people realise and deeper than policymakers are willing to admit. The problem will not be solved without a dedicated will and firm action by the state because solving it through market forces (while using state benefits to support private renting) is patently failing.

I've said a lot about the problems and I've suggested throughout this book improvements that should be made, but now I'm going to be more specific about what I think should be done. In the next chapter I'll put a timeline on this.

Firstly, we have to drop vague goals of 'building 300,000 homes a year' without specifying what kind of homes they should be and where they should be located. Homes are being built every year, but they are doing little to help people in housing need and may indeed be adding to the problems in an area, pushing house prices ever further out of people's reach.

Secondly, we need to abandon the cherished British idea of home ownership being the Holy Grail, to which everyone must aspire. Home ownership is right for many, but making it the priority form of housing tenure, with a high home-ownership rate being some sort of symbol of national pride, has led to the needs of non-homeowners – a growing and significant proportion of the population – being ignored and dismissed.

To make any real difference to housing need in this country, there has to be a large-scale building programme: our goal should be 3m homes over the next 10 years. That's 300,000 homes a year – but they should be homes to let at genuinely affordable rents and available on secure, long-term tenancies.

Whether we call this social housing or give it an alternative name (such as community housing, perhaps) if we think 'social housing' carries some sort of stigma, the principle must be that it is good-quality housing let at rents that can be fully covered by people's earnings or benefits. I stress *genuinely* affordable because 'affordable' has become a deceptive term in the way it is currently used, designating homes let at rents or sold at prices which are a very unaffordable 80% of market prices.

Providing social housing at scale is the only way to make a real impact on the housing need that is blighting people's lives now. We need it at a volume that gets people off waiting lists and out of bad housing within a few years. Every year that we don't act is dragging people, the economy, the nation's health and children's futures, further down.

This housing needs to be available on rental agreements that allow people enough security to plan their lives. It has to be built in places where people need homes, near work and schools, and the properties must be built to last and to high standards of energy efficiency and sustainability, so that maintenance costs and households' utility bills are lower. There will need to be a mix of housing for all types of households – single people, families, and with provision for our ageing population so that older people can live independently for longer in their own homes.

These developments will also offer an opportunity to contribute more to communities, as they can be designed to include green space, units for community facilities such as GP surgeries, and also the kind of affordable-rent retail and industrial units that small businesses are crying out for and which, crucially, provide local jobs.

There are a great many community groups, planners, architects, engineers, and others out there who already have ideas on how to do this and expertise to offer. There are examples of successful modern developments in Europe and some, on a small scale, in Britain.

Is this feasible? Yes, if we adopt the right mindset and learn from the mistakes of the past.

It calls for the proactive approach of the early new towns and council estates: the idea that ordinary people deserve decent homes and decent local facilities. It also calls for an acknowledgment that the state must take the lead.

Local authorities are currently in a weakened state after years of having to make deep budget cuts, but they are still the bodies best placed to assess housing need and land availability in their areas, and to do so democratically, accountable to local residents, so they must be central to this enterprise. Powers must be returned to them so that they can borrow money and hire the qualified people needed to manage these projects.

It may be that many councils will want to work with housing associations or some other not-for-profit body, which is fine as long as these bodies are ethically run and not hand-in-glove with private developers. What we don't want are any Private Finance Initiative-type deals with commercial developers: time and again these have been shown to deliver nothing but a massive cost to the public purse, with huge profits taken by the private sector partners.

There will be no need for private investment if the deals are handled correctly.

Starting at ground level

First of all, the land. Councils must be able to buy land at prices that enable affordable rents. That is why, as happened with the early new towns, the land must be bought at current use values, not with the huge premium bestowed by planning permission. The vastly lower price of land will make it financially viable for the resulting housing to be let at genuinely affordable rents.

There is enough land already earmarked for housing to enable a social housing programme to begin straight away.

In addition to the land banks of 1.15m plots of land *with* planning permission that developers were sitting on in 2020, the Local Government Association (LGA) estimated that another 1m homes could be built on land already earmarked by councils for housebuilding, where the land had been banked by developers and no planning permission yet applied for.[1] In 2020, the LGA said this represented an additional 4.4 years' worth of housing supply, on top of schemes already granted planning permission or under construction.

The inadequate supply of homes in this country belies the fact that, behind the scenes, a massively profitable trade in potential housing land goes on. In 2018, *The Guardian* reported that: 'Companies known as strategic landowners make money for investors by buying agricultural land that may be needed for future housing at low prices, securing planning consent and selling it on for significant profits.'[2]

This tells me that the land is there, and the possibilities exist for work to start on building social housing without delay. Furthermore, in some areas there will also be, as explained in the previous chapter, available land belonging to public sector or brownfield sites ready for development. I've already mentioned the land owned by the Church of England.

Local authorities should be allowed to assess where would be the right sites for social housing and borrow the money to purchase (compulsorily purchase if necessary) the land they have identified at existing value, in other words, without the 'hope' value conferred by its being designated for development.

Inevitably, the relatively small number of landowners counting on selling their land for lucrative developments at vast profits won't like this change to the status quo, but they have had things their way for a long time and have made handsome returns from the current situation. They have essentially been given these fantastically valuable state assets (the planning permissions) for free. Also, some pension funds have made large investments in land banks precisely because of their profitability and will no doubt complain that 'pensioners will suffer' as a consequence of these much-needed reforms. But, again, they have made easy money from the current situation and should be looking for ethical investments elsewhere, as opposed to buying state assets on the cheap.

Local authorities will issue planning permission to themselves and either design and manage the project in-house or work with competent, ethically run housing associations. There would need to be a fast-tracked programme of recruitment and training to do this, as most councils' experienced teams have long been wound down.

Construction would be carried out by building contractors, who would make their profit out of doing the work rather than from the planning permission gain. The effects for the building industry would be favourable: builders would simply be constructing social housing rather than private housing and would benefit from an increased, and regular, flow of work.

The financial savings of doing it this way would be staggering. For example, the cost of building a quality flat or small family house in quantity, using good materials, is around £100,000, plus another £50,000 per unit to cover landscaping, highways access and connection to services in the development. These figures are excluding land costs, which would be a tiny element if the 1961 Act were repealed. With the 'cost' of this money on the money markets at 5%, the interest to finance this accommodation would be less than £150 per week. In addition, there would be maintenance and management costs, but even taking these into consideration at an estimated £30 per household per week, the net result could be rents significantly less than what households are currently paying in private rented accommodation (typically at least £250 a week). If the social landlord decided to set rents lower, any shortfall would be more than covered by the enormous rise in asset values, with the land cost being so low.

When you consider that £102bn was spent on housing benefit between 2016 and 2020, a vast amount of which was effectively taxpayers' money going into the pockets of private landlords, it's clear that the savings to the public purse would be immense over time. In addition, the state would benefit from the capital growth, with the publicly owned housing stock being an asset increasing in value over time.

Quality construction

For the building industry, this programme should mean a big boost in profitable work, with knock-on benefits to the economy. That said, it needs to be recognised that there is a serious skills shortage and, occasionally, a materials shortage for the construction industry in the UK, which makes it all the more important to approach this programme in a coordinated way and ensure that training and apprenticeships are put in place asap.

Good-quality, responsible building firms will benefit: the losers will be the large-scale developers, who make their profits from planning gain. Some builders are also small-scale local developers, but there is nothing to say that private developments will grind to a halt because of the social housing programme. People will still want to buy new houses. I do expect though that the building of homes for private renting will dwindle.

I would emphasise that it is essential that all the

construction and associated businesses benefitting from this massive expenditure programme are socially responsible – the definition of which would include not employing workers on zero-hours contracts, being signed up to the Living Wage Foundation[3] and the Fair Tax Mark[4] and, ideally, being Good Business Charter-accredited. A project designed to bring social benefits cannot be allowed to cheat society by being used as an opportunity for dodging tax and exploiting employees.

Realistically, the target of 3m homes will take a time frame of 10 to 15 years to deliver, with probably three years to get fully up to speed. This should be achievable, given that 2.8m homes were built in the 1950s and 3.6m in the 1960s using relatively primitive building techniques. Modern methods of construction should be employed to speed up production and ensure good design and environmental best practice. We will need to plan for fast-track construction in large quantities so that the economies of scale are realised, but without cutting corners. The lessons of the 1960s and 70s – when some horrendous mistakes in construction were made because of cost cutting (and, in places, corruption involved) – must be learned.

The other crucial lesson we should learn is to futureproof these homes. For years now there's been a missed opportunity to ensure that newly built homes have the build quality, the insulation, and the necessary technology to make them low carbon and cheap to heat. The benefits, to the residents and to the climate, are obvious. It is a scandal that housebuilders have got away with not making new homes energy efficient simply because they did not want to invest the money. Back in 2015, the government scrapped regulations requiring housebuilders to ensure all new homes were low carbon, so, not surprisingly, few developments are built to good eco standards. In an investigation in October 2023, *The Guardian* reported that: 'The construction sector saved at least £15bn since 2015 by building homes to old, high-carbon standards, without solar panels and batteries, heat pumps and effective insulation.'[5]

Residents get hit twice: firstly with higher energy bills and secondly with the potential future cost of the property having to be brought up to environmental standards. *The Guardian* reported that, for the builder, the cost of incorporating higher standards of insulation and such items as solar panels and heat pumps would be around £8,500, whereas the cost to the homeowner for retrofitting these things would be around £33,000, not to mention difficult and disruptive.

As with all big projects, the execution of our large-scale developments is paramount. The very best management should be sought – people with proven track records of success in large capital projects, and they should be monitored and rewarded relevantly and accordingly. Ongoing inspection will be key. Councils' building control departments must be strengthened to ensure that standards are kept to and corners are not cut.

Does the public sector have the capacity to manage this scale of capital project? There are over 300 housing authorities, made up of city or unitary councils and district councils. Some districts are rural and relatively small: they may have a good knowledge of the housing need in their area, but not the capacity to tackle it. One idea might be to create, say, 10 regional centres of excellence, perhaps with the involvement of housing associations. While they will be able to respond to their regional needs, they should be controlled centrally so that performance is being monitored and so that best practice can be rolled out for everyone's benefit.

From my experience in business, I know this is the most efficient approach and it prevents people having to continually reinvent the wheel in multiple locations to solve problems. Admittedly, it would mean a completely new managerial infrastructure being built from scratch, which might also cause delay, but it could also boost councils' buying power and permit economies of scale. Alternatively, in many parts of the country, neighbouring district councils have already banded together to run some services jointly, thereby saving money, so perhaps they could form housing consortia.

Can the nation afford it?

No doubt one of the first objections to an expansion of social housing will be the claim that the nation can't afford to spend the money. I think we can. For a start, we would be borrowing to invest in a fast-growing asset for the state, one which also delivers revenue in terms of rent.

Secondly, this objection ignores the fact that the state already spends enormous sums on supporting the private housing market.

The *UK Housing Review*, an annual publication by housing experts, analysed the planned government support for affordable and private market new-build investment in England for the period 2021-22 to 2024-25.[6] The figures for that four-year period show a spend of £17.2bn on 'affordable rent' housing and low-cost home-ownership schemes. It's a complex picture, with a plethora of grants, loans and guarantees (and remember that 'affordable' schemes are rarely affordable for anyone on a lower income). The £17.2bn includes grants of nearly £10bn and loans of £4.5bn.

This is a substantial sum that will be spent without – I would argue – offering any help to people in real housing need.

A much larger sum goes on support for private sector housebuilding and house purchases. The government's Home Building Fund provides development finance to small and medium housebuilders and infrastructure funding to support large developers and landowners. These are loans intended to help businesses that cannot get development finance on the private market. The aim is 'to bolster housebuilding and diversify the market', the government says. The Home Building Fund, Help to Buy loans and ISAs, plus other initiatives, add up to £37.6bn for the period, of which £17.5bn is in grants. More than £8bn is allocated to Help to Buy schemes for the four-year period.

When we add these sums to the billions spent on housing benefit, it's no good pretending that the state can't afford to help people with their housing. It's just that this spend is not making a dent in housing need. Schemes supporting home buying are not means-tested and mostly help those with incomes above £40,000. Help to Buy has generally pushed up property prices, making huge profits for developers in the process, and has increased private renting far more than home ownership. There has been nothing to stop profiteering by people who bought with this subsidy and then sold on rather than live in the property. Meanwhile, the scheme has been of no use to key workers and other working households unable to get a mortgage on these overpriced properties.

These schemes should be cancelled. The money would be far better spent on providing genuinely affordable social housing and, if small and medium-sized builders and developers are profitably employed building this new social housing, they will not need government loans.

Compare all this expenditure with the idea of 3m social rented homes, costing £150,000 each to build, plus modest land costs (if the 1961 Act were repealed). In cash flow terms this would be £45bn per year over 10 years – an absolute bargain compared to other capital projects. More importantly, the value of these attractive homes would be far more, creating a huge capital profit for the state, plus the income stream from rents.

A social housing programme made to last

New social housing projects springing up all over the country will be very visible to communities, so it is paramount that fairness is seen to operate. As this new housing becomes available (and let's get the ball rolling quickly by bringing empty homes back into use, as well as building new ones) the obvious priorities would be to house people on the local authority waiting list and to get homeless families out of temporary accommodation and into a place of their own. The financial savings to local authorities will be quickly apparent.

As supply increases, however, the aim would be to have enough social rented housing that there is no longer any need to ration it to the most needy and it could become the housing of choice for a wide range of people, including young, single people.

Attitudes to home ownership have already shifted among younger generations. This is hardly surprising when many of them have had to come to terms with the idea that the price of houses puts home ownership permanently out of reach for them. They've also seen how buyers have stretched themselves so far to get a mortgage that the rise in mortgage interest rates was a disaster for them, so I think that many will see affordable, secure, social renting not as second-best but as a positive choice.

Let's get away from the idea that good-quality, social rented housing is something that must be 'deserved'. Those who can afford it will pay the full rent – they won't be receiving any kind of handout. Those on low incomes or not working will get the welfare support they qualify for, as now. Whether this is in the form of housing benefit or some other kind of support for their rent could be up for discussion.

The obvious point is that with the rents on social housing being so much lower than private sector rents, there will be a huge saving to the state's welfare bill because we are taking profit out of the rent equation and all the capital growth of the properties will go to the state.

A mix of tenants should be part of the new developments from the start, so schemes for different types of social housing for different needs should be part of this model, including both communal and supported housing. There should be housing designed to suit elderly people, people with disabilities, victims of domestic violence, people with mental health needs, ex-offenders and so on – all kinds of groups that are currently crying out for homes that would enable them to live better lives.

There should also be the flexibility for any tenant

to move easily as their circumstances change, but, on the whole, we want these to be people's homes for the long term.

There is no need for the tenancies to be restricted in terms of length because, unlike private landlords who may want to sell their property at some point, the social housing landlord is in it for the duration. So I would suggest a straightforward and flexible tenancy, letting tenants remain for as long as they require, subject only to their paying the rent and not breaking the terms of their tenancy agreement through anti-social behaviour.

On the subject of rents, I think we should be prepared to consider fresh ideas. One proposal that I think is worth further consideration would be to have, say, several bands of rent. Tenants whose household income is low would be on the lowest band; if and when their circumstances improved in more prosperous years of their lives, they would rise up the bands. If their income drops, say, due to unemployment, sickness, or retirement, they could drop down the bands accordingly.

To give a very broad-brush example of how this might work, if we take our basic, newly built house or flat, costing the state £150 a week in debt servicing, residents who are unwaged or below Living Wage Foundation rates might be charged £50 a week (paid for via benefits if necessary). Key workers or those on low salaries with household income below £30,000 might pay £100 a week, those with household income between £30,000 and £50,000 might pay £150 a week and those with a household income over £50,000 might pay £200 a week.

Local authorities would want to set their own bands in the light of incomes in their area. The bands could be tapered to make the steps in rent more gradual and they must also be proportional to the size of the property. A simple way around this would be to have a multiplier of times one for an agreed 'fair-size' flat or house based on credible floor areas and then a corresponding uplift or reduction in the multiple for those that are different.

An approach like this has the virtue of simplicity and could avoid some of the pitfalls that currently exist with the interaction between rents and the benefits system. It is not the norm to link rents to income rather than the property, but I would like to think the higher rents would become aspirational in a good way, that tenants, as they prosper, would be proud to pay the higher rents as a sign of their success in the community. These rents will still be way below private-sector levels, so people who start earning more will have no need to move. The upshot will be more diversity of circumstances on social housing estates, which used to be the case but has been lost in the past 30 years, plus greater social cohesion as people stay longer in their homes.

However, I do acknowledge this is a complex issue and deserves proper discussion.

At the very least, the rents should be set at

Local Housing Allowance (LHA) levels (while they still apply). This will prevent the current situation where tenants claiming benefit become increasingly impoverished because they have to top up the rent payment with money they must find from other areas of their lives, as the LHA means their benefit falls short of their actual rent.

One thing we don't want is for these properties to be lost to Right to Buy. This new stock would not be subject to the Right to Buy (and residents would be aware of that when they took on the tenancy). We want these to be permanent additions to the country's social housing stock, not an opportunity for people to cash in at the taxpayers' expense.

The other lesson to be learned is the importance of management and maintenance, so that new estates don't degenerate in ways we've seen in the past. A further point (a lesson from the Grenfell disaster) is that tenants must have an effective voice in the management of their homes.

My observation on management, based on my experience of management in business, is that the key is getting the right balance between carrot and stick: setting out clear rules in the tenancy agreement, enforcing the rules – in particular, not allowing tenants to build up arrears and not tolerating serious anti-social behaviour – while providing a consistently good service and being responsive to the tenant's needs. This all sounds obvious but, in practice, it requires a lot of alert and proactive management, plus a commitment on the landlord's side to get repairs, maintenance and improvements done and to listen to what tenants are saying. The outcome is better for everyone because most people are reasonably law abiding. No one likes paying rent, but what people object to even more is seeing neighbours get away with not paying rent and trashing their property.

Transforming the housing situation in this country can be done because it's been done before. By the mid 1960s, huge numbers of people were living in clean, modern homes, a world away from the slums they had grown up in. It happened because the political will was there to do it.

Imagine if the construction of even 100,000 social homes a year were started, instead of the miserable current figure of less than 10,000. Within a few years, the supply of social housing would be increased to the extent that it was no longer residual housing confined to the most needy. Local authorities would be able to house people on their waiting lists, as well as homeless applicants. There would be a much greater range of types of households living in social housing and much greater opportunity for young people to create a home.

The quality of the stock would improve, and we would be gradually building a supply of housing ready to face the future. Research has shown the extent to which poor-quality housing is bad for people on so many levels: damp, uninsulated homes create ill health and leave residents at the mercy of high heating costs. Numerous housing factors are harming people's mental health: overcrowding, vulnerability to crime, poor access trapping them in their homes, fear of eviction because of insecure tenancies, the sheer misery of living in a crumbling building. So, conversely, imagine what good housing would do for people's physical and mental health. The capital investment would repay itself many times over in the benefits to society and also in vast savings to the public purse.

CHAPTER 10

Time for action – my housing manifesto

In my business, I always distinguish between ideas and execution. When we have a challenge, we first need suggestions for how to tackle it. We don't rule any out on the grounds of 'that won't work' because making things work or not is to do with execution.

Throughout this book I've talked about a lot of ideas on how to resolve aspects of the housing disaster, and there are many more out there. But what about the execution? Coming up with ideas is the easy bit: making them work is the difficult stuff.

But that should not be a reason to do nothing. Action is needed urgently: the housing disaster has been growing since the Right to Buy came in 40 years ago and has accelerated drastically in the last 20 years. With every year that passes, it blights society further and builds up problems for the future. It is affecting people's health, damaging the economy, obstructing our ability to cope with the climate crisis and, most importantly, ruining individuals' lives. This includes children's lives because, with every year of inaction, children growing up in bad housing, or even homeless, are suffering the effects to their health and education.

A general election is looming and I'm calling on politicians of all parties to make housing a priority and to be ready to take bold decisions that will have real results.

The housing disaster has been created by the whole of society, in truth, because of what we've prioritised and what we've neglected, but the crucial decisions must be taken by the state. Solving our deep-seated housing problems calls for everyone to adjust their mindset and get away from our tunnel-vision focus on home ownership as being the sole form of housing to be validated by society and supported by government.

Tackling the disaster requires action not only by government departments, but also by landlords, local authorities, landowners, housing associations, businesses and many others who have the power to make changes.

A new mindset is needed:

1. To see good-quality social housing as currently the best way out of our housing crisis, instead of looking for market-based solutions;

2. To regard social renting as a valid option for people from all walks of life;
3. To see responsible renters (private and social) as being equally important and as worthy of protection as homeowners;
4. To see the social housing stock as something that should be good quality, well-maintained and well-managed, not neglected on the assumption that tenants who have no choice cannot expect better;
5. To accept that people need somewhere to live and that well-planned, new, social housing can be an asset to communities and to society as a whole rather than an unwelcome imposition.

With all the actions I propose, it is vital that we learn the lessons from the past. The need for more social housing is urgent, but we must be aware that a nationwide rush to build could result in shoddy construction and dubious employment practices. If the country is going to invest in new housing, the stock should be built to last and constructed to meet high environmental standards, which will save residents money, reduce carbon consumption, and make the homes fit to face future environmental pressures. This calls for not only good design but also for robust inspection to ensure that standards are met and that the taxpayer is getting value for money.

So where should we start? Here's what I think a realistic timeline looks like for my top 20 urgent fixes:

Short-term actions

1. Improvement in the private rented sector can be started without delay. A Responsible Landlords Charter, as I propose in chapter 6, should be created to benefit both tenants and good landlords. This is something landlords can sign up to themselves, with no need to wait for a change to the law. If the response to this suggestion is favourable, I will consider setting this up myself (on similar lines to the Good Business Charter).
2. Implement the reforms to landlord/tenant law that are already in the pipeline. Changes proposed in the Renters (Reform) Bill have met with broad approval from renters and housing experts. They should be implemented with immediate effect, especially the banning of section 21 'revenge' evictions and allowing longer-term tenancies to enable families to plan their lives. Priorities for reforms are:
    - Assured Shorthold Tenancies (AST) to be able to be extended for up to five years by mutual agreement, with rent increases linked to the retail price index.
    - The only reasons for eviction within these ASTs should be non-payment

of rent or anti-social behaviour by the tenants.

- Clear responsibilities for tenants set out in tenancy agreements, so that landlords can act fast against anti-social behaviour and negligent rent arrears.
- Statutory inspection of private-sector rented properties, with local authorities having the power to close down unsafe and unsanitary ones. The extended inspection regime would be funded by landlords paying a fee to the local authority, in order to be inspected and approved.

3. Scrap government-subsidised home-ownership schemes with immediate effect. These are an unnecessary burden on the taxpayer, they push up prices and do nothing for the less well-off in society (see chapter 9).
4. Allow local authorities to reinvest the proceeds of current Right to Buy sales in social housing.

Medium-term actions

5. Repeal the Land Compensation Act 1961. This must be repealed as an absolute priority in order to allow public authorities to buy land without the 'hope value' premium so

that social housing development can go ahead, as I explain in chapter 7.

6. From the outset, implement training programmes to address the current shortage of skilled workers in the building industry.
7. Lift financial restrictions on councils so that they can borrow the money to invest in buying land and building social housing. Only public investment will deliver genuinely affordable homes, not public/private partnerships or Private Finance Initiative deals that have proved to be a bad deal for the taxpayer.
8. Scrap the Right to Buy in England. It has already been abolished in Scotland and Wales. As a priority, have no Right to Buy on new social housing developments. This is essential to stop new homes leaking out of the social housing sector only a few years after they have been built, all at a cost to the taxpayer. It will also end the deterrent for ethical investors to invest in social housing (because they have no wish to fund housing that will ultimately be lost to the sector). The Right to Buy completely undermines efforts to drive up the volume of social housing for rent.
9. Reform the planning permission process. Planning permission must no longer be given away. It is a valuable state asset that

must be priced accordingly for developers, as I've proposed in chapter 7, with local authorities able to invest the proceeds in social housing. The handling of planning permission must be a closely monitored and transparent process, with zero tolerance of corruption within planning authorities.

10. Scrap section 106 agreements, which have failed to deliver significant levels of social benefits or affordable housing. Ensure that the proceeds of Community Infrastructure Levies are genuinely invested in infrastructure that benefits residents.
11. Put a moratorium on planning permission for private developments where there is a high need for social housing.
12. Tighten up the law on permitted development to ensure it is not misused to allow shoddy housing.
13. Ban offshore trusts and companies from buying property or land, unless the beneficial owners are disclosed and funds proven to be legitimate and tax paid.

Longer-term actions

Important steps are needed to get 3m homes for social renting built over the next ten years. Some will require legislative change. Some of these reforms are complex and will require expert input and transparent discussion.

14. Allow councils to review land that already has planning permission for homes but has not yet been built on and enable them to compulsorily purchase it for social housing.
15. Councils should also be allowed to purchase plots which have been landbanked and do not yet have planning permission. This would also have the benefit of preventing landbanking profiteering going forwards.
16. Require public bodies and landowners, such as the NHS and the Church of England, to assess their land holdings and commit to making a proportion available for social housing (otherwise their surplus land could also be subject to compulsory acquisition).
17. Set quality standards for sustainable housing so that homes are built to last and to meet the demands of the future.
18. Have inspections rigorously carried out during construction to ensure standards are met.
19. Require local authorities to work with ethical builders who meet standards of good business practice.
20. Carry out an analysis of how to set truly affordable rents fairly, possibly with different bands proportionate to income and, in turn, reduce the housing benefit bill.

Conclusion

Our housing disaster has been years in the making and it will take years to address. I realise the long-term nature of this process poses difficulties for politicians who are reluctant to plan beyond the usual four-year electoral cycle, but we cannot bring about a fairer housing system for our citizens without long-term thinking.

It won't be easy because housing need is acute right now, and assuring people that things will be better in 10 years' time is not going to win any votes. On the contrary, preparing for a 10-year project of social housing development risks raising expectations and thereby causing disappointment and frustration if people feel they are no nearer to getting the home they desperately need.

But doing nothing is not the answer, and making vague promises while leaving the market to supply the homes is definitely not the answer either. Successive governments have relied on these approaches and the crisis has only got worse.

The large-scale development of social housing that I believe is necessary will take several years to come on stream. There will be a long gestation period: much needs to be done before the first foundations are dug. Plans have to be drawn up, land identified and bought, more construction workers will need to be trained, local authority planning, building regulation and other departments need to be resourced and strengthened. Good architectural and engineering design needs to go into these developments if we are to have new housing that lasts.

All these things are possible with the right will and investment, but they will take time. They also demand cross-party co-operation at local and national level if politicians are not to rip each other's plans apart and start again every time there is a local or national election.

If politicians can be bold enough to make the initial key decisions, after three years we'd see a big ramping-up of social housing output, but a real meaningful time period has to be 10 years. It's a long time, but it would be 10 years of doing something rather than doing nothing.

Moreover, while we are making these long-term plans, short-term improvements can be quickly made. Reforms to the private renting sector have cross-party support and can be put in motion straight away; responsible landlords can act even sooner to make changes themselves, with the help of local authorities, as I've suggested.

We do have the funds to put into improving housing, and these can be found speedily, given the political will. Allowing the proceeds of Right to Buy sales to be re-invested in social housing would make a big difference. Scrapping government financial support schemes for home ownership would also free up money for social housing and help get homeless families out of temporary accommodation.

The longer-term issues, such as repealing the Land Compensation Act and allowing councils to carry out compulsory purchases of land are much tougher. These measures will clash with vested interests, including, no doubt, property-owning MPs and members of the House of Lords. I would urge them to vote with their citizen's hat on rather than in consideration of their personal interests.

The level of housing need in this country is acute and the only real solutions lie through politics. The housing disaster can only be addressed through a change in mindset, a resetting of national priorities and action at the highest level. The crisis calls for a rethink of the assumptions that policy has been based on for more than 20 years. It calls for decisive action by government to make changes in legislation and invest in people and assets. It also calls for a willingness at all levels to tackle the complex, messy business of managing expectations and balancing competing interests, which in a democracy are part and parcel of creating change for the better.

References

Introduction

[1] https://www.independent.co.uk/news/uk/politics/mortgage-house-prices-labour-reeves-b2371815.html

Chapter 1

[1] https://www.nationwidehousepriceindex.co.uk/reports/house-price-growth-shows-signs-of-stabilisation-in-april
[2] https://www.ons.gov.uk/peoplepopulationandcommunity/personalandhouseholdfinances/incomeandwealth/bulletins/householddisposableincomeandinequality/financialyearending2022#:~:text=Main%20points,(ONS)%20Household%20Finances%20Survey
[3] https://ifs.org.uk/books/barriers-homeownership-young-adults
[4] https://www.thisismoney.co.uk/money/mortgageshome/article-11671251/Average-time-buyer-deposit-62-500-Halifax-data-shows.html
[5] https://www.gov.uk/government/statistics/english-housing-survey-2021-to-2022-headline-report/english-housing-survey-2021-to-2022-headline-report
[6] https://www.bbc.co.uk/news/61407508
[7] https://www.theguardian.com/money/2004/mar/17/business.housing
[8] https://www.bbc.co.uk/news/business-42055623
[9] https://publications.parliament.uk/pa/ld201617/ldselect/ldeconaf/20/20.pdf
[10] https://www.nao.org.uk/wp-content/uploads/2023/07/dwp-report-on-accounts-2022-23.pdf
[11] https://www.housing-ombudsman.org.uk/2024/01/23/ombudsman-calls-for-royal-commission-to-re-establish-housing-policy
[12] https://news.leicester.gov.uk/news-articles/2022/november/city-council-declares-housing-crisis/

[13] https://www.housing.org.uk/globalassets/files/report-people-in-housing-need-final.pdf
[14] https://www.archbishopofcanterbury.org/sites/abc/files/2021-02/coe-4794-hcc-full-report-v6.pdf
[15] https://www.ons.gov.uk/peoplepopulationandcommunity/populationandmigration/populationestimates/bulletins/populationestimatesforenglandandwales/mid2022
[16] https://www.refugeecouncil.org.uk/information/refugee-asylum-facts/top-10-facts-about-refugees-and-people-seeking-asylum/

Chapter 2

[1] https://england.shelter.org.uk/support_us/campaigns/social_housing_deficit
[2] https://www.gov.uk/government/statistics/social-housing-sales-and-demolitions-2021-22-england/social-housing-sales-and-demolitions-2021-22#:~:text=In%20 2021%2D22%20there%20were%2024%2C932%20 sales%20of%20social%20housing,owned%20by%20 private%20registered%20providers. and https://www.gov.uk/government/statistical-data-sets/live-tables-on-affordable-housing-supply
[3] https://www.gov.uk/government/statistics/english-housing-survey-2021-to-2022-headline-report/english-housing-survey-2021-to-2022-headline-report
[4] https://www.bma.org.uk/news-and-opinion/damning-survey-results-reveal-scale-of-junior-doctors-hardship
[5] https://www.economicsobservatory.com/how-does-the-housing-market-affect-uk-productivity
[6] https://www.theguardian.com/society/2023/dec/31/uk-housing-ombudsman-failing-to-fine-housing-associations-for-mould

[7] https://www.theguardian.com/money/2024/jan/20/councils-in-england-inspect-only-half-of-all-mould-reports-in-private-rental-housing#:~:text=The%20Observer-,Councils%20in%20England%20inspect%20-only%20half%20of,reports%20in%20private%20rental%20housing&text=Budget%20cuts%20mean%20local%20councils,)%2C%20the%20Observer%20can%20reveal.

[8] https://www.theguardian.com/society/2022/nov/15/around-120000-families-in-social-housing-in-england-have-mould

[9] https://www.england.nhs.uk/2023/01/nhs-pressure-continues-as-hospitals-deal-with-high-bed-occupancy/

[10] https://bregroup.com/press-releases/bre-report-finds-poor-housing-is-costing-nhs-1-4bn-a-year/

[11] https://www.theguardian.com/society/2023/oct/27/councils-in-england-paying-17bn-a-year-to-house-people-in-temporary-homes

[12] https://www.bbc.co.uk/news/articles/c5173znwp8jo

[13] https://www.theguardian.com/society/2023/oct/20/more-english-councils-face-bankruptcy-leaders-warn-as-deficits-reach-4bn

[14] https://assets.ctfassets.net/6sxvmndnpn0s/3sMXwT7ruuGfQFipEIRyYn/185b9d87080a10dee48942c4bfc04ae2/Still_Living_in_limbo_Exec_Summary.pdf

[15] https://www.gov.uk/government/statistics/social-housing-lettings-in-england-april-2021-to-march-2022/social-housing-lettings-in-england-tenants-april-2021-to-march-2022

Chapter 3

[1] https://www.schroders.com/en-gb/uk/individual/insights/what-174-years-of-data-tell-us-about-house-price-affordability-in-the-uk/

[2] https://connect.open.ac.uk/money-business-and-law/britains-housing-crisis

[3] https://www.ons.gov.uk/peoplepopulationandcommunity/birthsdeathsandmarriages/families/bulletins/familiesandhouseholds/2022#:~:text=Households-,There%20were%20an%20estimated%2028.2%20million%20households%20in%20the%20UK,both%202012%20and%20in%202022.

[4] https://www.shu.ac.uk/centre-regional-economic-social-research/publications/profits-before-volume-major-housebuilders-and-the-crisis-of-housing-supply

[5] https://www.local.gov.uk/about/news/housing-backlog-more-million-homes-planning-permission-not-yet-built

[6] https://www.gov.uk/government/news/cma-finds-fundamental-concerns-in-housebuilding-market

[7] https://bcis.co.uk/news/housebuilding-cost-inflation-eases/#:~:text=Annual%20housebuilding%20cost%20inflation%20as,of%201.7%25%20recorded%20for%204Q2022.

[8] https://lordslibrary.parliament.uk/meeting-housing-demand-built-environment-committee-report/#:~:text=Help%20to%20buy%20scheme.&text=The%20committee%20said%20it%20had,spent%20on%20increasing%20housing%20supply%E2%80%9D.

Chapter 4

[1] https://www.theguardian.com/society/2017/dec/08/right-to-buy-homes-owned-private-landlords

[2] https://www.ons.gov.uk/peoplepopulationandcommunity/housing/bulletins/privaterentalmarketsummarystatisticsinengland/april2022tomarch2023

[3] https://www.gov.uk/government/statistical-data-sets/live-tables-on-rents-lettings-and-tenancies

[4] https://www.uswitch.com/mortgages/buy-to-let-statistics/#:~:text=%C2%A38.5%20billion%20worth%20of%20buy%2Dto%2Dlet%20properties%20were,mortgage%20lending%20for%20the%20year.

[5] https://www.theguardian.com/politics/2023/may/04/hunt-and-braverman-among-five-in-cabinet-earning-thousands-as-landlords

[6] https://www.theguardian.com/society/2017/nov/20/one-in-seven-councillors-in-english-rental-hotspots-are-landlords
[7] https://www.gov.uk/government/collections/homelessness-statistics Table A
[8] https://theindependentlandlord.com/latest-renters-reform/
[9] https://www.local.gov.uk/parliament/briefings-and-responses/renters-reform-bill-committee-stage-house-commons-7-november
[10] https://england.shelter.org.uk/media/press_release/no_fault_eviction_court_proceedings_hit_seven-year_high
[11] https://www.gov.uk/government/statistics/english-housing-survey-2021-to-2022-headline-report/english-housing-survey-2021-to-2022-headline-report#section-2-housing-stock

Chapter 5

[1] https://www.versobooks.com/en-gb/products/332-municipal-dreams and https://municipaldreams.wordpress.com/about/
[2] https://www.gov.uk/guidance/capital-funding-guide/10-right-to-acquire
[3] https://novaramedia.com/2023/08/04/its-a-scandal-how-property-developers-failed-to-sell-a-single-flat-in-balfron-tower/
[4] https://www.ons.gov.uk/peoplepopulationandcommunity/housing/datasets/dwellingstockbytenureuk
[5] https://www.islingtontribune.co.uk/article/after-16-years-of-pfi-control-of-homes-is-taken-back-in-house
[6] https://www.theguardian.com/uk-news/2024/jan/15/asylum-accommodation-to-be-excluded-from-social-housing-landlords-crackdown
[7] https://asbhelp.co.uk/
[8] https://www.theguardian.com/housing-network/2012/aug/15/tom-manion-reward-society-housing

Chapter 6

[1] https://www.gov.uk/guidance/guide-to-the-renters-reform-bill
[2] https://goodbusinesscharter.com/
[3] https://fairnessfoundation.com/issues/housing
[4] https://www.ons.gov.uk/peoplepopulationandcommunity/housing/bulletins/privaterentalmarketsummarystatisticsinengland/october2022toseptember2023
[5] https://www.savills.co.uk/insight-and-opinion/savills-news/354578/uk-rents-to-keep-on-rising-but-will-hit--affordability-ceiling--in-2025
[6] https://www.smith-institute.org.uk/wp-content/uploads/2020/11/MakingHousingAffordableAgainFullreport.pdf
[7] https://ifs.org.uk/publications/housing-quality-and-affordability-lower-income-households
[8] https://england.shelter.org.uk/media/press_release/814000_private_renters_under_threat_of_eviction_this_winter_
[9] https://www.rics.org/news-insights/market-surveys/uk-residential-market-survey
[10] https://www.citizensadvice.org.uk/housing/renting-privately/during-your-tenancy/dealing-with-repairs/
[11] https://www.unison.org.uk/news/2019/04/environmental-health-cuts/#:~:text=environmental%20health%20budgets%20per%20head,between%202009%20and%202018)%3B
[12] https://www.tradingstandards.uk/news-policy-campaigns/news-room/2023/ctsi-and-cieh-issue-joint-response-to-fsafss-report-on-local-authority-workforce-capacity-and-capability/
[13] https://www.nao.org.uk/press-releases/investigation-into-supported-housing/
[14] https://publications.parliament.uk/pa/cm5803/cmselect/cmpubacc/1330/report.html#:~:text=The%20Committee%20concluded%20that%20some,to%20make%20profit%20from%20it%E2%80%9D.

Chapter 7

[1] https://whoownsengland.org/

[2] https://labour.org.uk/updates/press-releases/how-not-if-labour-will-jump-start-planning-to-build-1-5-million-homes-and-save-the-dream-of-homeownership/

[3] https://www.hbf.co.uk/news/number-of-new-homes-gaining-planning-permission-continues-to-plunge/

[4] https://www.gov.uk/government/statistics/planning-applications-in-england-october-to-december-2022/planning-applications-in-england-october-to-december-2022

[5] https://www.gov.uk/government/news/communities-put-at-heart-of-planning-system-as-government-strengthens-levelling-up-and-regeneration-bill

[6] https://www.ons.gov.uk/peoplepopulationandcommunity/housing/bulletins/housingaffordabilityinenglandandwales/2022

[7] https://www.oecd.org/cfe/cities/land-value-capture.htm#:~:text=Land%20value%20capture%20is%20a,action%20should%20generate%20public%20benefit.

[8] https://www.landcommission.gov.scot/downloads/5dd6a24c0c1d6_Land-Focus-Land-Value-Capture-May-2018.pdf

[9] https://neweconomics.org/2022/02/how-private-developers-get-out-of-building-affordable-housing

[10] https://www.gov.uk/government/publications/national-planning-policy-framework--2

[11] https://www.theguardian.com/artanddesign/2022/oct/05/every-square-inch-monetised-battersea-power-station-playground-super-rich

[12] https://www.gov.uk/guidance/community-infrastructure-levy

[13] https://assets.publishing.service.gov.uk/media/5a815b06e5274a2e8ab538c3/CIL_Research_report.pdf

[14] https://www.london.gov.uk/programmes-strategies/planning/implementing-london-plan/mayoral-community-infrastructure-levy

[15] https://labour.org.uk/wp-content/uploads/2019/06/12081_19-Land-for-the-Many.pdf

Chapter 8

[1] https://www.gov.wales/50m-bring-empty-homes-back-life
[2] https://emptyhomespartnership.scot/
[3] https://commonslibrary.parliament.uk/research-briefings/sn03012/
[4] https://www.mortgagesolutions.co.uk/news/2023/02/23/empty-homes-in-england-near-700000-leeds-bs/
[5] https://www.theguardian.com/environment/green-living-blog/2010/oct/14/carbon-footprint-house
[6] https://www.actiononemptyhomes.org/News/national-empty-homes-week-2023-sees-call-for-action-on-one-million-homes-nobody-lives-in
[7] https://www.gov.uk/government/statistics/uk-stamp-tax-statistics/uk-stamp-tax-statistics-2021-to-2022-commentary#main-points
[8] https://www.london.gov.uk/mayor-london-and-westminster-city-council-call-stronger-powers-crack-down-long-term-empty-properties
[9] https://www.bbc.co.uk/news/articles/c976lzzz1pno
[10] https://www.dailymail.co.uk/property/article-11973211/Londons-homes-65-properties-plush-city-centre-unoccupied.html
[11] https://www.theguardian.com/uk-news/2023/nov/20/london-billionaires-row-derelict-site-affordable-homes-architects-blueprint#:~:text=Now%2C%20Britain's%20leading%20architects%20have,homes%20on%20one%20particular%20site
[12] https://www.bbc.co.uk/news/articles/cw89g46p6dxo
[13] https://oneworld-publications.com/work/the-great-tax-robbery/
[14] https://www.taxwatchuk.org/
[15] https://www.theguardian.com/business/2018/oct/24/why-a-liverpool-tower-block-was-a-magnet-for-foreign-capital
[16] https://www.gov.uk/government/news/build-on-brownfield-now-gove-tells-underperforming-councils
[17] https://bpf.org.uk/media/press-releases/bpf-comment-on-secretary-of-states-announcement-on-housing-delivery-and-new-consultation-on-permitted-development-rights-1/

[18] https://www.bbc.co.uk/news/uk-england-essex-47720887
[19] https://www.theguardian.com/society/2023/nov/18/england-nature-chief-tony-juniper-thinks-green-belt-land-solve-housing-crisis#:~:text=England's%20nature%20chief%20calls%20for%20building%20on%20green%20belt%20to%20solve%20housing%20crisis,-Tony%20Juniper%20believes&text=Building%20on%20the%20green%20belt,space%2C%20England's%20nature%20chief%20says.
[20] https://www.theguardian.com/politics/2014/oct/19/is-it-time-to-rethink-the-green-belt
[21] https://www.theguardian.com/politics/2024/jan/02/green-belt-building-design-tsar-nicholas-boys-smith
[22] https://neweconomics.org/2020/02/sold-off-public-land-is-creating-minuscule-amounts-of-affordable-housing#:~:text=For%20almost%20a%20decade%2C%20the,5%20billion%20in%20capital%20receipts
[23] https://www.property.nhs.uk/services/property-disposals/
[24] https://neweconomics.org/2019/06/houses-built-on-nhs-land-sold-for-up-to-9-6-times-the-average-nurses-salary
[25] https://www.nhshomesalliance.co.uk/

Chapter 9

[1] https://www.local.gov.uk/about/news/developers-yet-seek-planning-permission-more-million-earmarked-homes-lga-research
[2] https://www.theguardian.com/politics/2018/feb/01/labour-plans-landowners-sell-state-fraction-value#:~:text=Companies%20known%20as%20strategic%20landowners,it%20on%20for%20significant%20profits
[3] https://www.livingwage.org.uk/
[4] https://fairtaxmark.net/
[5] https://www.theguardian.com/politics/2023/oct/04/at-least-one-tenth-tory-donations-since-2010-property-industry#:~:text=The%20construction%20sector%20%E2%80%93%20including%20some,heat%20pumps%20-and%20effective%20insulation.
[6] https://www.ukhousingreview.org.uk/ukhr23/housingexpenditure.html